SHINING
BIG SEA
WATER

SHINING BIG SEA WATER

THE STORY OF LAKE SUPERIOR

NORMAN K. RISJORD

MINNESOTA HISTORICAL SOCIETY PRESS

Lyrics on pages 145–46: "The Wreck of *Edmund Fitzgerald*." Words and music by
Gordon Lightfoot. © 1976 (Renewed) Moose Music Ltd. All Rights Reserved.
Used by Permission of Alfred Publishing Co., Inc.

Front cover: View of Lake Superior and sky at Isle Royale National Park.
Philip Schermeister, National Geographic. Courtesy Getty Images.
Back cover: Loading giant freighters at ore docks on Lake Superior, MHS collections.
Cover design: Dennis Anderson

www.mhspress.org

The Minnesota Historical Society Press is a member of the
Association of American University Presses.

Printed in Canada

10 9 8 7 6 5 4 3 2 1

∞ The paper used in this publication meets the minimum requirements of the
American National Standard for Information Sciences—Permanence for Printed
Library Materials, ANSI Z39.48–1984.

International Standard Book Number 13: 978-0-87351-590-0 (paper)
International Standard Book Number 10: 0-87351-590-0 (paper)

Library of Congress Cataloging-in-Publication Data

Risjord, Norman K.
Shining big sea water : the story of Lake Superior / Norman K. Risjord.
p. cm.
Includes bibliographical references and index.
ISBN-13: 978-0-87351-590-0 (pbk. : alk. paper)
ISBN-10: 0-87351-590-0 (pbk. : alk. paper)
1. Superior, Lake—History. 2. Superior, Lake, Region—History.
3. Superior, Lake, Region—Social life and customs. I. Title.
F552.R57 2008
977.4'9—dc22
2007042926

To my grandfather, Gulick N. Risjord,
state circuit judge in
Ashland, Wisconsin, 1912–52

CONTENTS

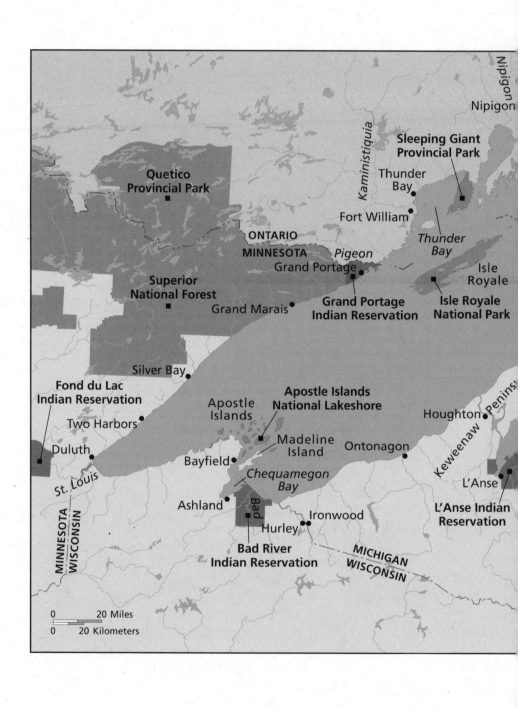

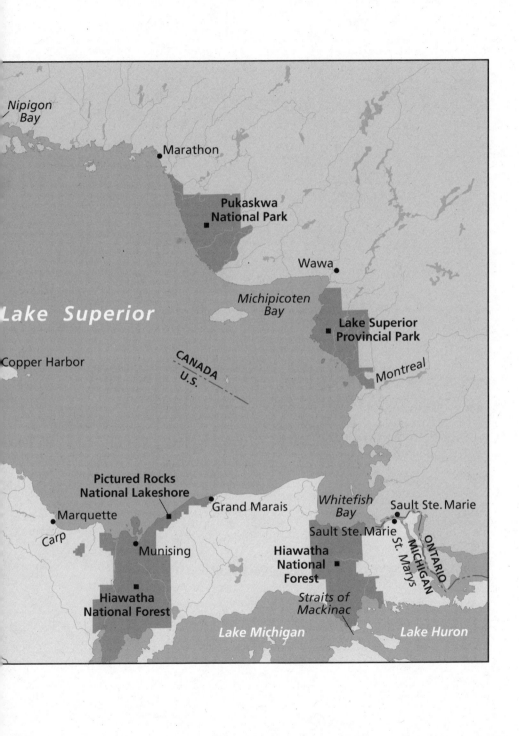

Nipigon
Bay

Marathon

Pukaskwa
National Park

Wawa

Michipicoten
Bay

Lake Superior

Lake Superior
Provincial Park

Copper Harbor

CANADA
U.S.

Montreal

Pictured Rocks
National Lakeshore

Marquette

Carp

Munising

Hiawatha
National Forest

Grand Marais

Whitefish
Bay

Sault Ste. Marie

Sault Ste. Marie

Hiawatha
National
Forest

St. Marys

ONTARIO
MICHIGAN

Straits of
Mackinac

Lake Michigan

Lake Huron

PREFACE

THIS BOOK was a labor of love. In my childhood I spent many happy hours wading—never able to fully immerse myself—in the icy waters of Lake Superior on the beach at Ashland, my grandfather's home. When our own sons were able, at the ages of four and six, to make their first camping trip (sleeping in the back of a station wagon), my wife, Connie, and I took them around Lake Superior. I shall ever remember a moonlit night in a tiny campground at the falls of the Baptism River in Minnesota. In doing the final research for this book, Connie and I made a second trip around the perimeter of the lake. We were aided in this quest by a superb guidebook, Hugh E. Bishop's *Lake Superior: The Ultimate Guide to the Region* (2005).

The idea for a cultural history of Lake Superior was actually that of Greg Britton, then the director of the Minnesota Historical Society Press and now publisher for the J. Paul Getty Trust. This is the third of my books to be inspired by Greg. Ours has been a long and very productive friendship. As in the past, I owe a huge debt of gratitude to the superb editorial staff of the Minnesota Historical Society Press and to the many excellent suggestions of its unnamed reviewers.

My greatest thanks, however, go to my wife, Connie: my most resourceful editor and fearless critic.

NORMAN K. RISJORD
Middleton, Wisconsin

SHINING
BIG SEA
WATER

CHAPTER ONE

OF BEDROCK AND ICE

LAKE SUPERIOR, the largest freshwater lake in the world, displays its geological past to good effect. Its irregular shoreline of bays, inlets, and peninsulas; the colorful palisades of rock on Ontario's north shore; and Michigan's dramatic Au Sable Dunes are footprints from the march of time.

Billions of years ago, the earth was a mixture of water and rocky land-masses that were proto-continents or what geologists call *cratons*. The cratons were rooted in the earth's mantle (the superheated rock between the crust and the molten core), and parts of them periodically sank into the mantle to be metamorphosed with the addition of new elements, such as nickel, cobalt, and magnesium. One of these cratons, formed about 2.5 billion years ago, extended from present-day Greenland, across eastern Canada, and as far as central Michigan, Wisconsin, and Minnesota. Known as the Canadian Shield, this mass of granitic bedrock can be seen today in the cliffs along Lake Superior's north shore or where it has been scraped bare by the glaciers of the past two million years.

Rooted in the unstable magma, the cratons moved around over millions of years due to plate tectonics. Shortly after the Canadian Shield was formed, it collided with other cratons, creating a "supercontinent" that included northern Asia and much of today's Europe. About 2.1 billion years ago the North American craton fragmented along a line that roughly parallels the south shore of present-day Lake Superior and the north shores of lakes Michigan and Huron. The seas swept in, and for several million years Wisconsin and Michigan lay under water. The lands around this arm of the sea—still without vegetation—eroded, and sand was washed into the shallow water, accumulating in some places to a depth of several hundred feet. Under heat and pressure it hardened into sandstone; if the folds of the earth brought it closer to the hot magma, it solidified into quartzite. When the land rose out of the water (due to another craton collision), the newly fashioned sedimentary rock formations emerged. The sandstone can be seen today in the red cliffs at the tip of the Bayfield Peninsula, and it is the basic rock of the Apostle Islands. The quartzite hills around Marquette, Michigan, are remnants of the metamorphosed sandstone.

The sedimentary rocks that materialized from the shallow sea in northern Michigan, Wisconsin, and Minnesota contained large deposits of iron ore. The origin of this ore remains somewhat a mystery. Ore-bearing sediments accumulated around the world at the same time, about two billion years ago. There are no iron ore deposits from an earlier or a later period. The best explanation for this phenomenon is the presence, for the first time, of oxygen in the atmosphere. Single-celled plants had appeared almost as soon as the oceans were formed, and these blue-green algae were capable of photosynthesis, the process of converting the atmosphere's carbon dioxide into free oxygen. The oxygen joined nitrogen in the atmosphere and was dissolved into the ocean. Iron is quite soluble in oxygen-deficient waters and would have been present in large quantities in the earliest oceans. With the oxygen it formed ore compounds—hematite, pyrite—that are insoluble. The precipitates collected in depressions at the bottom of the sea and later emerged as iron ranges in Michigan, Wisconsin, and Minnesota.

About 1.8 billion years ago a craton drifted up from the south (possibly after splitting off from Africa) and collided with the Canadian Shield craton, forming an arc from southern Ontario across northern Michigan and Wisconsin and southwest to the Minnesota-Iowa border. The intruding craton slipped under the Canadian Shield, creating an enormous volcanic uplift which, after eons of weathering and erosion, can be seen today in Iron Mountain, Michigan, and the Northern Highland

The picturesque markings of Michigan's Pictured Rocks are created by mineral-rich water seeping through cracks in the sandstone cliffs. Wave action has bored caves in the softer sandstone. The layers were created by the interaction of land and water billions of years ago.

of Wisconsin. Geologists believe this ancient mountain range might, at one time, have been as high as the present Rockies.

The final chapter in the geological formation of the basin that would become Lake Superior was a cataclysmic event that began about 1.1 billion years ago and ended a hundred million years later. It began with a rift in the landmass that had become the continent of North America. The break—resembling the continental rift in East Africa today—was several hundred miles wide and in the shape of an arc with the pinnacle being the basin of Lake Superior. One arm stretched southwest down the St. Croix valley, across Minnesota and Iowa, and into central Kansas. The other arm reached across Michigan and ended near its border with Ohio. Basaltic lava spewed to the surface along this rift and pillowed in

 **VISITING HISTORY**

Red Cliff (Ojibwe) Indian Reservation (Highway 13 north of Bayfield, Wisconsin) features immense cliffs of red sandstone on the lake's shore.

Ouimet Canyon Provincial Park (Highway 11/17 about forty miles east of Thunder Bay, Ontario) encloses a five-hundred-foot-deep canyon that provides a spectacular view of the billion-year-old Laurentian Shield.

The North Shore Drive (Duluth to Two Harbors, Minnesota), a National Scenic Byway, is an alternative to four-lane Minnesota Highway 61. In addition to beautiful vistas of the lake, the byway features the North Shore's ancient basalt formations. The scenic drive can be continued on Highway 61 from Two Harbors to Grand Portage.

The Sleeping Giant (Highway 11 and Ontario 587, Thunder Bay, Ontario) is a basalt rock formation on the Sibley Peninsula that forms the eastern side of Thunder Bay. It is part of a one-hundred-square-mile Natural Environment Park whose Visitor Center and a two-hundred-site campground are on Marie Louise Lake, the largest of several glacial remnants on the peninsula.

The "sleeping giant" rock formation at the tip of Sibley Peninsula, Ontario, was created by basaltic lava during the Earth's distant past. From right to left: the giant's head, Adam's apple, chest, waist, and knees. In the foreground is Marie Louise Lake, one of Glacial Lake Superior's many remnants on the Sibley Peninsula.

some places to a height of one or two miles. Toward the end of this volcanic period the land that is now the Lake Superior basin subsided, but several spectacular features remained: the basaltic ridge known as the Keweenaw Peninsula of Michigan and the basalt cliffs along the northwest shore of the lake from Duluth to Grand Marais. Other remnants are Isle Royale and the Sleeping Giant on Thunder Bay, its eight-hundred-foot sheer cliff the highest on the north shore.

Copper deposits were another remnant of the Keweenawan eruption. As the lava cooled and fissured, superheated water brought copper and nickel sulfides to the surface, and the solutions settled into crevices of the cooling rocks. The most important deposits were on the Keweenaw Peninsula and on Isle Royale. Although much of the copper was in the form of an ore (with oxygen and sulfur), nodules of almost pure copper were left on the surface, particularly on the Keweenaw. Lake Superior agates were another product of the volcanic eruption. As the lava cooled, silica and iron oxides washed into cavities in the basaltic rock. Variations in the amount of iron and silica released at any one time produced the banded layering that makes agate one of the loveliest of semiprecious stones.

About 570 million years ago, the southern half of the North American continent sank once again under the sea. Water covered present-day Michigan and the eastern corner of Lake Superior. The rest of the future lake bed, the northern half of Wisconsin, and nearly all of Minnesota remained above water, although the landscape was still barren. The continent straddled the equator at that time, with today's Thunder Bay crossed by that imaginary line, and the warm seas swarmed with the first animals—worms, snails, and, most abundantly, crablike creatures only an inch or so in size, trilobites. By the time the seas retreated for the last time about 250 million years ago, ferns and mosses covered the land, insects had made their appearance, and reptiles including dinosaurs had begun to evolve.

While the seas were advancing and retracting throughout this three-hundred-million-year period, the North American tectonic plate collided with the Eurasian one, creating a supercontinent (Gondwanaland), which allowed the intercontinental exchange of animals, including dinosaurs and the first mammals. The supercontinent began to break up about two hundred million years ago, and a narrow Atlantic Ocean separated Europe and America by about one hundred million years ago.

Grasses made their appearance about this time, and the basin that would become Lake Superior was probably a grassy plain surrounded by the highlands created by the Keweenawan eruption. The basin drained into a northward flowing river that led ultimately to the Arctic Ocean. Until two million years ago, when the most recent glacial age, the Pleistocene, began, the climate of North America was much warmer than at present, and its woods and grasslands sustained an abundance of animal life. Horses, which originated in North America, were common, and they shared the prairies with mammoths, camels, an ancestor of the rhinoceros, and various carnivorous predators, including the famed saber-toothed tiger. All of these large animals would become extinct toward

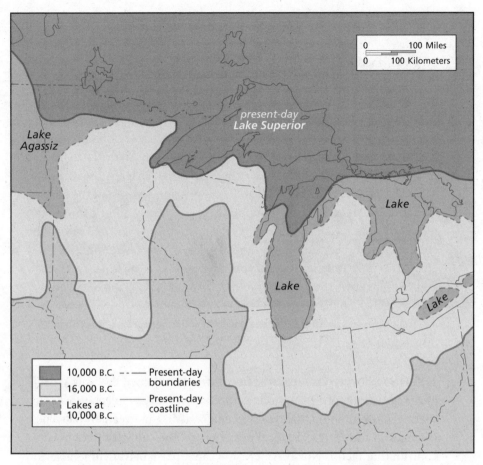

The glaciers that covered the region that would become Lake Superior extended as far south as today's central Iowa and Illinois but bypassed a large segment of Wisconsin.

the end of the Ice Age, though some, like the horse and the camel, would migrate to Asia before their relatives in North America vanished.

The Wisconsin Glacier

According to geologists, although numerous glacial advances occurred in North America over the last two million years, the one responsible for the birth of Lake Superior was the most recent one, called the Wisconsin glaciation because of its impact on the topography of the Badger State. Many theories set out the causes of glaciation. The movement of tectonic

J. Elliot Cabot's 1848 sketch *Lake Terraces* makes visible the different levels of lakeshore as Lake Minong receded to present Lake Superior.

plates (South America separated from Africa and joined the New World at the beginning of this period, 2.5 million years ago) affected oceanic thermal currents and thus caused major shifts in weather patterns. Changes in the earth's elliptical orbit around the sun may have been a contributing factor. North America became particularly vulnerable to the ice sheets as the Earth's axis tilted and the equator moved south to its present position, leaving two-thirds of the continent north of the 45th parallel.

When the climate cooled, winter snows in the Arctic failed to melt in the summer, and the snow accumulated year after year, century after century. The Wisconsin glaciation originated in two highlands, east and west of Hudson Bay, about seventy thousand years ago. At these centers, the snow eventually reached a height of almost two miles. Under this immense weight, the bottom layers recrystallized to form ice, which oozed and flowed with the incline of the land. When the two ice sheets joined, their weight was such that it dented the earth's crust, allowing the ocean to enter Hudson Bay after the ice melted. New snows replenished the mass, and the wall of ice crept south at a rate of about two hundred feet each year.

The moving ice gathered everything in its path, from giant boulders to sand and gravel. The debris added to the scouring effect, and the earth was laid bare to the bedrock of the Canadian Shield. When the advancing ice reached the wooded valley between the Minnesota and Wisconsin highlands, it split into lobes that followed ancient rifts and rivers. One lobe moved westward and plowed out the basin that would become Lake Superior. Another lobe moved southward along a river valley that would develop into Lake Michigan. Since much of the Lake Superior lowland consisted of sand and gravel that had eroded from the Wisconsin and Minnesota highlands, the glacier was able to plow deeply, gouging a lake bed that would reach seven hundred feet below sea level. (Lake Superior today reaches a depth of 1,300 feet.) For several thousand years, the Wisconsin highlands acted as a dam that prevented further movement to the south. As a result, the Superior ice lobe pushed westward into central Minnesota, where it halted when the climate began to warm.

The eastward lobe split into the Green Bay and Lake Michigan lobes, the first covering eastern Wisconsin, the second reaching into northern Illinois. To the south of these lobes, a tundra of moss and spruce parkland stretched to the Ohio River. Beyond, a spruce forest reached almost to the Gulf of Mexico, where it yielded to deciduous hardwoods.

The earth's climate began to warm again about eighteen thousand years ago. The ice halted its advance and began a stutter-step retreat from the Superior basin that lasted for another eight thousand years. The rock and gravel it had gathered was left in a succession of moraines and oblong hills called drumlins. The western half of Lake Superior was free of ice about thirteen thousand years ago and created in northern Wisconsin and northeastern Minnesota a glacial lake slightly larger than Lake Superior's current size. It drained south through the St. Croix valley, joining the re-forming Mississippi River west of the current Twin Cities. Lake Superior was completely ice free by about twelve thousand years ago, and the St. Marys River sent its waters south and east into lakes Huron and Michigan. As the glaciers gained ground about five hundred years later, the Superior basin refilled with ice, which stayed perhaps another fifteen hundred years. Once again ice free by about ten thousand years ago, the upper Great Lakes formed a giant freshwater sea that drained eastward through the Ottawa River and later southward into the present-day Chicago and Illinois rivers. And then, some two thousand years ago, bedrock rebounded at Sault Ste. Marie to separate Lake Superior from Lake Huron, and the contours of the present Great Lakes emerged.

In the wake of retreating ice, an arctic tundra comprising mosses, arctic grasses, dwarf birch, and willow covered the land. Spruce rapidly replaced the tundra and dominated the western shores of Lake Superior by about eleven thousand years ago. Large mammals including the woolly mammoth, the musk ox, and the caribou, able to withstand the cold, had moved onto the tundra even before the boreal forest appeared. As the climate continued to warm, spruce were forced north; white pine and then hardwoods such as birch, maple, and oak crept onto the shores of the great inland sea. About five thousand years ago the climate cooled to its present state, and spruce eventually dominated once again the forest on Superior's north side. Moose had moved into the late glacial spruce forest, and white-tailed deer thrived in the developing mixed forest south of the lake. Coldwater fish such as lake trout and whitefish began to colonize the inland sea, but other species such as bass, pike, and walleye did not appear until lake levels dropped and the waters warmed. As the glaciers retreated, the first human hunters arrived on the shores of the ancient Great Lakes.

The First Americans

When the Wisconsin glacier was at its peak, about twenty thousand years ago, so much of the earth's water was tied up in ice that the sea level was about three hundred feet lower than it is today. A thousand-mile-wide land bridge opened in the Bering Strait between Alaska and Siberia, separating the relatively warm Pacific Ocean from the frigid waters of the Arctic. Warm Pacific currents probably kept the bridge and the southern part of Alaska free of ice. Large mammals that had originated in Asia or Africa crossed to North America—the grass-eating mammoth, the brush-eating mastodon (both relatives of the elephant),

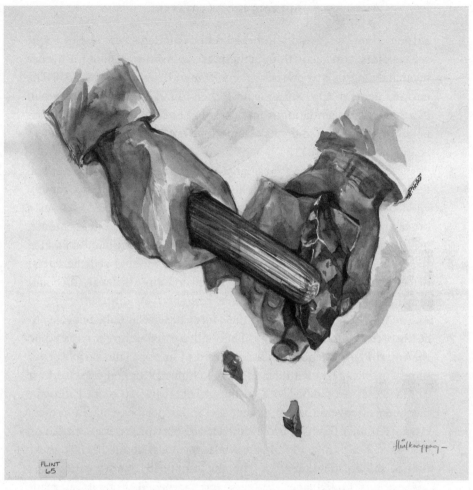

Flintknapper by P. Hefko shows one technique used to make prehistoric stone tools.

the giant sloth, and the saber-toothed cat—while American-born horses and camels crossed the bridge into Asia. Also crossing over, perhaps as early as twenty thousand years ago, were human hunters, pursuing the large beasts on which they had subsisted in Asia.

Moving south along the Pacific Coast or along a de-glaciated gap on the east side of the Rocky Mountains, the first Americans occupied much of the southern part of North America by eleven thousand years ago. These earliest settlers have been identified by a distinctive tool, a spear point chipped out of flint or chert that was hollowed out ("fluted") at the butt end so it could be fastened to a wooden shaft. These unique spear points (unlike anything then in use in Asia) were first uncovered by archaeologists at a site near the village of Clovis, New Mexico. The encampments of Clovis people have been found at numerous places in North America, all dating from 13,500 to 12,900 years ago. The Clovis people never occupied the Lake Superior basin due to glacial ice and an uninviting environment.

By the end of Clovis times, large mammals in North America had undergone a massive die-off. Mammoths, mastodons, horses, camels, giant beavers, and saber-toothed cats all became extinct. Curiously, other sizable species survived, including bison, elk, caribou, moose, grizzly bears, and white-tailed deer. Some researchers have attributed the extinction to human hunting; others have emphasized the effects of climate change. Until scientists uncover more evidence, the issue remains unresolved.

The first humans arrived on the shores of Glacial Lake Superior by at least ten thousand years ago. Their culture apparently originated on the Great Plains; hence they are referred to as the Plano people. They hunted using spears with dart heads of chipped stone, similar to those of the Clovis people but without fluted butts. An important Plano site has been discovered about twenty-five miles northeast of the present city of Thunder Bay, Ontario. Named the Brohm Site, it was situated on the gravel beach of a glacial lake whose level was about 230 feet above that of present-day Superior. The site contained characteristic Plano spear points, knife blades, scrapers, and sharpened choppers, all made of chipped stone, mostly from the iron ore taconite. The Planos' principal hunting quarry was probably caribou or elk; the lake waters were still too cold to sustain a catchable fish population.

Little evidence of a distinctive Plano culture exists after about ten thousand years ago. Newcomers from the south or west probably formed what archaeologists call the Archaic culture. An early stage— "Shield Archaic"—spread throughout the Canadian Shield, adapting to the gradually lowering waters of Lake Superior. They continued to hunt elk and caribou, but they also developed weapons and tools for hunting bear, beaver, and waterfowl. Prime among these was a spear-thrower, the atlatl, that doubled the throwing arc of the human arm and elbow.

A deer or rabbit effigy mound outlined with lime and photographed in 1914 was likely made by members of the Woodland Culture.

As the lake waters receded and warmed, fishing became an important part of the economy. The Shield Archaic people used fishhooks made of bone, nets and traps of wood sinew, and barbed harpoons.

During the later Archaic, from about 4,500 to 3,000 years ago, a subculture of Old Copper people appeared along the shores of Lake Superior. They mined copper on the Keweenaw Peninsula and Isle Royale and at various sites along the north shore. Beginning with the surface outcroppings, they dug pits that followed the copper veins, sometimes delving as deep as twenty feet. They broke off the copper-bearing rock with stone hammers, heated it over fire, chilled it with water, and split the copper free with wooden levers. Although they were some of the first fabricators of metal in the New World, the Old Copper people knew

VISITING HISTORY

Baraga County Museum (Baraga, Michigan), on the shore of Keweenaw Bay, contains exhibits of prehistoric cultures.

Isle Royale National Park is home to literally thousands of sites of the prehistoric copper culture, mostly remnants of shallow mines and fire pits where the people fashioned copper into tools and ornaments. The park is also a textbook display for geological formations, from primitive basalt to kettle-pond lakes deposited by the Wisconsin glacier

---

nothing of smelting and casting (bronze was being made in the Middle East by this time). Instead, they shaped the pure copper into tools and weapons by hammering while alternately heating and chilling it. Among their weapons were a variety of leaf-shaped knives and copper spear points with sockets for holding a wooden shaft. They also made copper adzes and axes with hollows for handles of wood or caribou antler. Household goods made of copper included needles, scrapers, drills, and spatulas apparently used in cooking.

The bow and arrow made its appearance in the Lake Superior region about fifteen hundred years ago. Likely of Asian origin, the concept—if not the weapon itself—may have been carried by people traveling by water after the seas covered the Alaskan land bridge. In Archaic times, dogs—perhaps also from Asia—arrived in the Lake Superior region. The Old Copper people had two kinds of dogs—one about the size of a coyote and a larger one similar to an Eskimo sled dog. Dogs were the only domestic animals kept by North American Indians prior to Europeans' arrival.

Skeletal remains of the Old Copper people indicate a physique similar to that of the Indians who greeted the explorers four thousand years later. They were fairly tall and had well-developed muscles, long heads, fairly high foreheads, and rather narrow faces. They buried their dead in cemeteries, arranging the bodies in set positions and providing them with tools, weapons, and ornaments for use in the spirit world.

The Old Copper people were followed by the Woodland tradition, usually exemplified by the Hopewellian culture that lived to the south. In the Superior basin, the Laurel culture (one to three thousand years ago) and its southern neighbor, the Blackduck culture (six to twelve hundred years ago), created pottery and followed the seasonal round, hunting deer, bear, moose, and beaver, fishing, and gathering foods such as wild rice. Unlike the Hopewells, they probably did not cultivate corn or other crops. They established winter camps and residential bases for warmer seasons, usually near water. The Woodland people are perhaps best known for their burial mounds, many of which were large and elaborate. The Laurel group left behind some of the earliest known ceramics of the Superior region.

Pottery shards and language similarities suggest extensive interchange among the Woodland Indians who lived between the St. Lawrence valley and the upper lakes. In early historic times, three major tribal clusters called the region home. The Algonquin occupied the St. Lawrence and Ottawa river valleys; the Ojibwe (or Ojibwa or Chippewa) centered on the eastern end of Lake Superior; and the Cree roamed the woodlands to the north. Their languages were similar, part of a family that anthropologists have termed *Algonquian*. Neighboring tribes also in this language family were the Potawatomi and Ottawa of present-day Michigan and the Menominee of northern Wisconsin. Pottery remains and a consistency of tools and weapons indicate considerable travel and trade among all these groups.

CHAPTER TWO

LIFE ALONG THE SHORE

THE SETTLEMENTS that France established along the St. Lawrence River in the early years of the seventeenth century had only one purpose—furthering the fur trade. The French government sent to the New World only traders and soldiers; the Catholic Church added a handful of missionaries. There were no women or children until the latter half of the century, when the youthful Louis XIV caught the fever of colonial empire. With furs in mind, colony governor Samuel de Champlain befriended the Algonquin people of the river valley and sent them to trade with the Woodland tribes farther inland. That action placed the French in the middle of a rare tribal conflict. The five nations of the Haudenosaunee—the Iroquois Confederacy—residing south of Lake Ontario (present-day western New York), were sworn enemies of the St. Lawrence Algonquin. Warfare escalated when the French used firearms to protect their Algonquin allies. The Iroquois' initial alarm at the sound of gunfire gave way to rage, and they began raiding the French settlements, nearly wiping out the trading post of Montreal.

Deprived of the use of lakes Ontario and Erie by Iroquois hostility, the French found a more northerly route to the western Great Lakes. The Ottawa River emptied into the St. Lawrence at Montreal, and from its headwaters a short portage led to waters that drained into Lake Huron. Astride this natural highway to the west were the Ottawa or Odawa, an Algonquian people whose very name translated as "trader." For years the sociable Ottawa had been the link between the St. Lawrence valley and the western lakes. Their reach extended west as far as Wisconsin, to the Siouan-speaking Winnebago or Ho-Chunk. They also traded with their neighbors to the south, the Wyandotte or Huron, who lived along the shores of the lake that bears their name. Of Iroquois language stock, the Huron resided in semi-permanent villages, and, like members of the Haudenosaunee, they tended gardens of corn, squash, and tobacco when growing seasons were adequate. The French absorbed both Ottawa and Huron into their trading system, and the two tribes became middle-men, swapping beads and blankets, occasionally even firearms, for furs, which they carried to Montreal.

In 1610, before the French clashed with the Iroquois, Champlain had sent a young protégé, Etienne Brulé, to live with the Huron and learn their language. Adapting to Huron ways, Brulé lived and traveled with them for many years. He was the first white man to describe Lake Huron, paddle Georgian Bay, and perhaps visit the Straits of Mackinac. Sometime around the year 1620, he told French missionaries that "above Mer Douce [the "sweet sea," Lake Huron] is another very great lake, discharging into it by rapids nearly two leagues broad." Brulé claimed the Indians had told him that this upper lake "has an extent of thirty days' journey by canoe." Brulé himself paddled along the shore far enough to visit a place where Indians were taking copper from a mine. Although Brulé was not always a reliable informant, details such as the copper mine suggest his tale was true, making him the first European to visit Lake Superior.

In 1634, Champlain learned from Huron traders of the Ho-Chunk, who lived on a great lake far to the west. Thinking these people might know of a water route across the continent, the governor sent another of his youthful protégés, Jean Nicolet, to find them. En route to a rendez-vous with the Ho-Chunk at Green Bay, Nicolet crossed Georgian Bay of Lake Huron and came upon a river (later named the St. Marys) flowing into the lake from the north. Venturing along the river, he came upon a settlement of people who spoke a language similar to that of his Ottawa guides. At the head of the river, the waters of Lake Superior cascade over a sandstone ledge and drop twenty-two feet in a rapids three-quarters of a mile long. The river flows on for another forty-five miles before emptying into Lake Huron. Discovering that the Indians of the river lived mostly on fish caught in the rapids, Nicolet called them *Saulteurs,* "people of the rapids."

Years later, a French missionary described their method of taking fish:

> It is at the foot of these rapids, and even amidst these boiling waters[,] that extensive fishing is carried on, from Spring until Winter, of a kind of fish usually found only in Lake Superior and Lake Huron. It is called in the native language *Atticameg,* and in ours "whitefish," because in truth it is very white; and it is most excellent, so that it furnishes food, almost by itself, to the greater part of all these peoples.
>
> Dexterity and strength are needed for this kind of fishing; for one must stand upright in a bark Canoe, and there, among the whirlpools, with muscles tense, thrust deep into the water a rod, at the end of which is fastened a net made in the form of a pocket, into which the fish are made to enter. One must look for them as they glide between the Rocks, pursue them when they are seen; and, when they have been made to enter the net, raise them with a sudden strong pull into the canoe. This is repeated over and over again, six or seven large fish being taken each time, until a load of them is obtained.

These Algonquian people lived in communities made up of extended families, and they were probably related to fishing clans that Nicolet and other Frenchmen found on Mackinac Island in the straits between Lake Huron and Lake Michigan. The Saulteurs that Nicolet visited in early summer were probably year-round residents on the river. In the autumn, when the whitefish run was greatest, their numbers were augmented by groups of Ottawa and Huron from Georgian Bay. There is no evidence that the Saulteurs raised crops, perhaps because of summer fogs and early frosts. They did, however, obtain corn and vegetables in trade with the Huron. As their numbers grew, apparently due to migrants from the St. Lawrence, the Saulteurs moved to the west and south, and resettlement gave them yet another identity in the French records. The people who spread west along the shores of Lake Superior eventually became known as Ojibwe (often translated as "puckered," a reference to the sewing on their moccasins; they call themselves *Anishinaabe,* "the people"). Another branch that moved south to settle on the eastern shore of Lake Michigan called themselves Potawatomi ("keepers of the fire"). These

Centuries after a missionary described the Saulteurs' fishing methods, natives near the Sault continued to fish while standing in canoes.

movements were both hastened and disrupted by the Iroquois, who in the late 1640s launched some of the most vicious warfare among Indians that North America has ever seen.

Refugee Settlements

In 1624 the Dutch founded the colony of New Netherland at the mouth of the Hudson River; that same year they established a fur trading post, Fort Orange (later Albany, NY), near the junction of the Mohawk River with the Hudson. Just as the French had made the Algonquian middlemen in the fur trade, the Dutch employed the Iroquois. Provided with firearms, the Iroquois made tributaries of the people living south of Lake Erie. When the Ohio Valley tribes resisted, the Iroquois killed the warriors and seized the women and children, adding to their own numbers by incorporating the captives into their family groups. By the 1640s, the Iroquois had decimated the peoples living on the north side of lakes Ontario and Erie; in 1648 they attacked the villages of the Huron and Potawatomi. Remnants of these tribes fled across Lake Michigan to Green Bay. Ottawa refugees joined them when the Iroquois raids reached the Straits of Mackinac. Iroquois pressure south of the lakes pushed Ohio Valley tribes—the Miami, Sauk, and Fox—north and west into present-day Wisconsin.

In the mid-1650s, increasing population on the western shore of Lake Michigan, together with lingering fear of the Iroquois, sent a band of Huron fleeing west to the Mississippi River. They received there an un-friendly reception from the Dakota (or Sioux, whom the French called "the Iroquois of the West"), and within a year or so the Huron relocated again. They chose the one location east of the Mississippi that had no year-round inhabitants—the south shore of Lake Superior. Not surpris-ingly, they were soon joined there by remnants of their onetime neigh-bors, the Ottawa and Potawatomi.

In 1659 the fur trader Pierre Esprit Radisson, the first European since Etienne Brulé to venture onto the waters of Lake Superior, came across an Ottawa village at the base of the Keweenaw Peninsula and mixed communities of Huron, Ottawa, and Potawatomi on Chequamegon Bay. Radisson and his partner, Medard Chouart Groseilliers, spent the win-ter at a village a few days' walk inland. Radisson did not identify the inhabitants of the village, but they were probably a mixture of Ottawa and Huron. As refugees, the Indians had little food in storage and little experience hunting a sterile forest of spruce and moss. Heavy snows added to their difficulties, and Radisson reported several hundred deaths by hunger before the spring thaw arrived and deer became trapped in the soft snow.

In 1665 Bishop Laval at Quebec, who had ecclesiastical jurisdiction over all of New France, sent the Jesuit Claude Allouez to establish a mission on Chequamegon Bay. Arriving there in September, Allouez described it as "A beautiful bay, at the bottom of which is situated the great village of savages, where they plant their fields of Indian corn, and lead a stationary life. They are there to the number of 800, bearing arms, but collected from seven different nations, who dwell in peace with each other." Besides Ottawa and Huron, Allouez noted a few Sauk and Fox, refugees, no doubt, of the Iroquois attacks near Lake Michigan. Although Allouez had little success in converting the Indians, who greeted his tales of holy spirits and resurrection with a mixture of disbelief and amusement, he explored the western shore of the lake extensively, reaching a Cree village on Lake Nipigon. He returned to Quebec in 1667 and was reassigned to the mission at Green Bay.

In 1669 Father Jacques Marquette arrived to carry on baptisms in the crude, bark-covered chapel that Allouez had erected on the southwest corner of the bay, about a mile from the main Ottawa village. Marquette remained at the mission, now named La Pointe de St. Esprit, for two years, during which the local Indians worked as middlemen between the French and the Dakota of the St. Croix and Mississippi river valleys. The Dakota resented this arrangement, wanting to trade directly with the French. Warfare erupted in 1670; according to the *Jesuit Relations*, annual missionary reports compiled in Quebec and published in France, the Huron/Ottawa started it. Fearing they would be overwhelmed by the numbers and ferocity of the Dakota and comforted by a momentary truce in the wars of the Iroquois, the Algonquian tribes fled eastward, the Ottawa settling on Mackinac Island, the Huron returning to their homeland on Georgian Bay. The effect was to leave the south shore of Lake Superior once again virtually uninhabited—a vacuum soon to be filled by the westward-moving Ojibwe.

Ojibwe Migration

In 1664 the English seized the Dutch colony of New Netherland, and that same year the French arranged a temporary peace with the Iroquois (although Iroquois raids in the Illinois country would continue until a formal peace ended their wars in 1701). Iroquois pressure was thus apparently not a factor in Ojibwe movement west. Nor did they abandon their early habitations, although the population at the eastern end of Lake Superior was much reduced: in 1641 visitors from a Jesuit mission on Georgian Bay estimated the settlement that they called Sault Ste. Marie at about two thousand inhabitants; twenty years later, when a Jesuit mission was established on the site, it numbered only 150.

The Ojibwe migration was peaceful on the whole, but steady. In 1659 Radisson reported an Ojibwe presence on the Keweenaw Peninsula; this situation was confirmed by other French traders three years later.

The early missionary outpost on La Pointe grew into a Catholic community on Madeline Island, served by this church in 1870.

Within another ten years they had moved into the settlements abandoned by the Ottawa and Huron on Chequamegon Bay. With French mediation, the Ojibwe negotiated a truce with the Dakota that lasted for several decades. The fur trade flourished during the time of peace, and early in the eighteenth century the Ojibwe took advantage of their access to French firearms to push westward beyond Superior and into present-day Minnesota.

Other bands of Ojibwe moved westward along the north shore of Lake Superior in the second half of the seventeenth century, but they were too few and too scattered to warrant the attention of French missionaries. No good harbors to sustain fishing villages exist on the lake's northeast shore, and the Ojibwe people probably lived in widely scattered family units, like their linguistic cousins, the Cree. In 1667 Father Claude Allouez visited the north shore and described the people there as "much more nomadic than any of the other nations, having no fixed abode, no fields, no villages; and living wholly on game and a small quantity of oats [wild rice] which they gather in marshy places." In the mid-nineteenth century, Andrew Blackbird, an elderly mission-educated Odawa and Ojibwe leader and writer, recalled scornfully that his people had always referred to the denizens of the north shore as "the backwoodsmen."

From the seventeenth century to the early nineteenth, the Ojibwe people would be the principal inhabitants of the Lake Superior shore.

Ojibwe Culture

William Warren, a grandson of Euro-American and Ojibwe leaders at the Sault, interviewed tribal elders and wrote a history of the Ojibwe people in 1852 that described the origins and migrations of his people, whose oral history had gone unrecorded by the Jesuits and later white historians. The bases of their social organization remained the village and the clan. The head of one of the Ojibwe bands who had remained at Sault Ste. Marie explained to the governor of New France in the 1690s: "It is not the same with us as with you. When you command, all the French obey and go to war. But I shall not be heeded and obeyed by my nation in a like manner. Therefore, I cannot answer except for myself and for those immediately allied or related to me."

It nevertheless seems likely that the westward movement strengthened clan organization. The relocation of a family or village, for instance, required some planning, particularly with respect to the food supply, and preparation for potential conflict. Bands of combative young men from other tribes were a constant danger. Although the principal villages of the Fox lay far to the south, their hunters roamed the north woods and sometimes laid claim to the shores of Lake Superior. Although the conflict never came to open warfare, the migrating Ojibwe were obliged to remain militarily alert. Settling a village and laying claim to the surrounding territory may have further enhanced social cohesion.

Among the Ojibwe and other Algonquian tribes, the clan was essentially an extended family with membership inherited through the male line. Since marriage among clan members was a cultural taboo, young males were obliged to seek wives in another clan. Children belonged to their father's clan. Grandparents and uncles helped raise children, freeing mothers for such activities as fishing, berrying, or curing hides and skins. Since a village often consisted of several clans, women had frequent contact with their blood relatives and often worked together in performing their subsistence endeavors.

Each clan identified itself by a totem (also spelled dodaim), an Algonquian word meaning "action," "heart," "nourishment," signifying a consanguine relationship. The totems were symbols of birds, fish, mammals, or reptiles that conveyed particular qualities of strength, prowess, or wit. Among the most respected clans for their leadership qualities were bear and marten among mammals and crane and eagle among birds.

The totems also had a religious significance. The Ojibwe believed in a supreme being, Gichi-Manidoo, creator of the world and giver of life. Prime among the gifts of Gichi-Manidoo are Father Sun and Mother Earth. The one provides illumination and warmth; the other sustains life with beauty and nourishment. Like a man and a woman the sun and earth are different, but jointly they give and uphold life; thus they are honored and thanked with prayer.

Having created the world and everything in it, Gichi-Manidoo oversees its workings but never interferes. The Ojibwe and other Algonquian tribes believed Gichi-Manidoo would not benefit them or judge them personally. The gifts bestowed by Gichi-Manidoo—the gifts of light and warmth and life—were gifts to all, and no individual could presume that he or she was a special beneficiary. According to Ojibwe scholar Basil Johnston, when men and women "opened their senses to the motions, sounds, and smells of the forests, mountains, winds, and skies by day and night . . . [they] opened their minds . . . to the works and presence of [Gichi-Manidoo]." The means by which humans could repay Gichi-Manidoo's generosity was "By giving and sharing one's goods, knowledge, experiences, and abilities with the less fortunate of their kin and neighbors." In addition, individual fortune, good or ill, could be affected by spirits ("Little Manidoos") that roamed the woods. These spirits, among other functions, conferred special gifts—such as speed, intelligence, agility, or leadership—on certain animals. In adopting an animal as a totem, an Ojibwe clan sought the benefits and attributes bestowed by that animal's manidoo.

The Ojibwe—indeed, Algonquian tribes generally—believed good health was a product of good behavior. The religious order Midewiwin— from *mino* ("good") and *daewaein* ("heart")—was an intertribal society composed of both men and women. Individuals who exhibited upright behavior and benevolence toward others were invited to join and admitted after personal examination. Increasingly complex knowledge was required at each stage of initiation, and the order's rites even today are undertaken with the utmost secrecy. The ethical code devised by the Midewiwin for their own guidance and that of others, summarized by Basil Johnston, would have sounded familiar to an early Christian or an ancient Greek:

> Thank Kitchi-Manitou for all his gifts;
> Honor the aged, for in honoring them you honor life and wisdom;
> Honor life in all its forms;
> Honor women, for in doing so, you honor the gift of life and love;
> Honor promises;
> Honor kindness;
> Be peaceful, courageous, and moderate in all things.

Persons who failed to live up to this ethical system were liable to punishment by the Windigo, the one truly evil spirit in the Algonquian pantheon. A man-eating giant, the Windigo lurked in the woods, particularly in the wintertime. Although a potential threat to all, the Windigo selected for its victims persons who had transgressed or indulged themselves to excess.

The Shoreline Economy

Ojibwe villages, where people congregated during the fall and winter months, were located on waterways, initially the shores of Lake Superior, later those of inland lakes and rivers. In late spring and summer, families left the village and spread into the woods for hunting and berry-picking. In both village and forest encampment, the Ojibwe lived in wigwams (from *wiigiwaam,* an Algonquian word meaning lodge or dwelling) that were easily constructed and transported. Either circular or oval in shape, the wigwam consisted of poles planted in the ground, brought together in arches, and tied with fibers stripped from the inner bark of basswood trees. They were covered with rolls of birch bark or, occasionally, mats woven of bulrushes.

Prior to Europeans' arrival, Ojibwe implements were formed of wood, bark, stone, or clay. They made spoons and ladles of wood and cooking

VISITING HISTORY

River of History Museum (Sault Ste. Marie, Michigan) contains a fine display of Ojibwe life and hosts periodic demonstrations of their handicraft skills.

The **Bad River Reservation** (Highway 2, Odanah, Wisconsin) cultural center and late-August powwow provide artifacts and pictures of Ojibwe life both prior to and on the reservation.

St. Louis County Historical Society (Duluth Depot Museum, Minnesota) displays thirty-six paintings by Eastman Johnson depicting Ojibwe life in the mid-nineteenth century.

Fort William Historical Park (off Highway 61, Thunder Bay, Ontario) contains a replica Ojibwe village where local tribal members explain wigwam construction and demonstrate traditional cooking and crafts.

Thunder Bay Historical Museum (Donald Street East, Thunder Bay, Ontario) holds an extensive collection of Indian artifacts, including the largest assortment of Indian beadwork in Canada.

Within **Lake Superior Provincial Park** (Highway 17, south of Wawa, Ontario) is the Agawa Rock, a cliff overlooking the lake that contains pictographs believed to be 100 to 150 years old. The site is reached by a spectacular but somewhat difficult hiking trail.

pots of birch bark (filled with water, birch bark does not ignite). The Ojibwe fired clay for a rough pottery, but rounded bottoms suggest the pots were used as food storage vessels set into the ground. Their knives, scrapers, and hatchets were made of chipped flint. Deer bones and horns were fashioned into needles, awls, fire-making drills, and fishhooks.

Women made all the clothing, primarily from deerskins. After being removed from the animal, the hide was soaked in water for several days and then stretched on a wooden frame. A woman scraped off the hair and rubbed animal innards on the hide to soften it with oil. Suspended in smoke from a smoldering fire, the hide acquired a golden yellow color. The women sewed the hides into clothing using a fiber drawn from stalks of nettles or with sinews made from deer or moose muscle tendons. The nettle-stalk fibers could also be woven into a soft cloth that women used for underwear. A single garment for an adult required two deerskins, one for the front and one for the back. Rabbit skins were highly prized for small children's caps and blankets.

Moccasins were fashioned from the hides of deer or preferably moose because of its thickness. Each piece of footwear was made of a single piece of leather with a seam at the heel and gathered in the front in a sewn "pucker." Moccasins for winter wear were made slightly larger so that a liner of muskrat or rabbit fur could be inserted.

The bow and arrow was the main implement for both hunting and warfare. Bows were made from hickory or ash saplings, usually about four feet in length. Men stripped the outer bark and soaked the piece in water to make it pliable. The finished bow could have either flattened or rounded surfaces. The strongest bow was carved flat on the outer surface and ridged on the interior. Bowstrings were made of spun nettle fiber or animal sinew. Arrows were fashioned from the straight stalks of shrubs, preferably from the Juneberry bush. Indians in North America generally used chipped flint for arrow points, but the Ojibwe often chose sharpened bone, especially for deer hunting. When hunting ducks and other waterfowl, they used arrows made of pine or spruce, which floated if they missed the target.

The Ojibwe traveled mainly by water, initially along the shore of Lake Superior, later by inland lakes and streams. The standard canoe, about eighteen feet in length, was capable of carrying six adults. Canoes were made of birch bark, cut in the spring from a felled tree. The oldest and largest trees provided the heaviest bark and longest pieces. Thwarts, crossbars, and ribs were whittled from branches of cedar. Split roots of tamarack or spruce were used to tie the wooden pieces together and to stitch the bark covering. Seams were made waterproof with pine or spruce pitch applied by wooden spatula. The resulting craft was strong

The Ojibwe wigwam is shielded by birch bark to keep the interior cool in the summer. Cattail-stem mats add another layer to retain heat during the winter months.

enough to bear the waves of Lake Superior and light enough to be carried across portages by two men.

The Ojibwe were accomplished at fishing—a year-round occupation for both men and women—well before they reached the waters of Lake Superior. The most productive time was in autumn, when lake trout and whitefish came close to shore to spawn. Then, the villages put up their winter supply. Women did the fishing, using nets made of nettle-stalk twine, knotted together and tied to one-foot pieces of wood set about a yard apart. They set the nets, sometimes fifty yards long, and sank them in the middle with stones. The fish preserved for the winter were gutted, dried in the sun for two days, and stored in clay pots. During the spring and summer, the men did much of the fishing using either hooks and bait or a spear. They made fishhooks of deer bone. They used rough fish—bullhead and catfish—for bait, capturing them in small streams with traps made of woven branches. In the spring, when the largest fish came into shallow waters to spawn, men speared them at night from canoes, the light of their torches dancing on the water.

Berries, corn, and garden-grown squash were the main herbal features of the Ojibwe diet until, in their westward movement, they came upon the beds of wild rice in the Kakagon Sloughs of the Bad River, just east of Chequamegon Bay. Because of their role in the fur trade, the Ojibwe no doubt were familiar with the grain; once they settled along Lake Superior's shore, they became the primary harvesters of this food source. The Menominee—their name from the Ojibwe *manoominiig*, "wild rice people"—lived on the river of that name, which flows through a delta of rice marshes into Green Bay (and forms part of the present-day boundary between Wisconsin and the Upper Peninsula of Michigan). The grain had been a staple of the Menominee diet for centuries. Although the Menominee laid no claim, in the European sense of land ownership, to the shores of Lake Superior, they hunted and traded there. In 1660 Radisson reported meeting "an ancient witty man" living with his family in a "cottage" on the lake. "They weare," wrote Radisson, "of a nation called Malhonmines, that is, the nation of Oats, graine [that] is much in [that] countrey."

The French reference to wild rice as "oats" was not far off the mark, for it was a grain that bore no relation to Eurasian rice, except that it

Wild rice is traditionally harvested with two people in a canoe:
one to steer and one to knock the kernels into the vessel.

grew in shallow, gently moving water. The grain grew about four feet tall
and ripened in late summer. A Jesuit missionary described the Indian
method of harvest:

> A little before it ears, [they] go in their Canoes and bind the stalks
> of these plants in clusters, which they separate from one another by as
> much space as is needed for the passage of a Canoe when they return
> to gather the grain. Harvest time having come, they guide their canoes
> through the little alleys which they have opened across the grain-field,
> and bending down the clustered masses over their boats, strip them of
> their grain.

The stalks were "stripped" of the kernels by beating with sticks. Europeans were sometimes critical of the seeming inefficiency of this method because some of the kernels were lost in the water. What they did not realize was that wild rice is an annual and the "lost" kernels were necessary for reseeding. Onshore, the gathered kernels were dried in the sun, parched by smoke or fire, hulled in a treading pit, and then tossed in the air to remove any lingering chaff. While some eastern Indians stored rice and dried berries in sacks hung in trees, the Ojibwe customarily stored their rice underground in skin containers. A favorite vessel was the skin of a fawn, which, according to travelers, held about two bushels of rice.

Like the westward movement, the encounter with wild rice seems to have stimulated clan governance. In the eighteenth century a Yankee traveler, Jonathan Carver, noted that each Indian family had its own allotment in the sloughs of the Bad River. The women marked their family parcels by binding the stalks in a particular way or with a special color of twine. Among the Menominee, the men who spoke most frequently at councils and led war parties were also the leaders who directed the rice harvest and settled disputes among families. The Ojibwe probably maintained a similar form of justice.

Wild rice was boiled in water; parched kernels required about a half hour of cooking time. It was—and is—eaten as a side dish with venison or duck or made into a stew with small game such as rabbit, squirrel, or raccoon. Wild rice is rich in carbohydrates, protein, and several of the B-complex vitamins. In the traditional Indian diet, it was more nutritious than any other item, whether animal, vegetable, or fruit.

Nutrition, and an accompanying improvement in health and longevity, might well explain the next century's rapid expansion of the Ojibwe into present-day Minnesota and the Canadian prairies; they simultaneously retained populous settlements on the lakes of northern Wisconsin and along the shores of Lake Superior.

CHAPTER THREE

THE FUR TRADE UNDER THREE FLAGS

"OTHER ALGONQUIAN TRIBES [are] still further away, who dwell on the shores of another lake larger than la mer douce [Lake Huron], into which it discharges by a very large and very rapid river; the latter before mingling its waters with those of our mer douce, rolls over a fall [sault] that gives its name to these peoples [Saulteurs], who come there during the fishing season. This superior Lake extends toward the Northwest." This notation by a Jesuit missionary living among the Huron Indians in the mid-1640s is the first use of the name *Superior* for the westernmost of the Great Lakes. Although no white man, with the possible exception of Etienne Brulé, had as yet visited the lake, the Huron had clearly provided the Jesuits with descriptions of it. The Iroquois wars decimated the Jesuit missions and delayed any further acquaintance with Lake Superior for a decade and a half. Then, in the year 1659, two French fur traders, Pierre Esprit Radisson and his brother-in-law Medard Chouart, Sieur des Groseilliers ("Lord of the Gooseberries," a playful reference to a tract of land he possessed on the St. Lawrence River), explored the lake and provided the first description of it.

Departing from their homes at Three Rivers in August 1659, the pair of Frenchmen paddled up the Ottawa River and its many portages to Lake Nipissing. Along the way they encountered a party of Huron who had delivered furs to Montreal and were returning to their homes at Green Bay and Chequamegon Bay. The Frenchmen accompanied the

Huron to Georgian Bay and enlisted several as guides and paddlers into Lake Superior. At some point they also obtained Ojibwe guides.

Leaving Lake Huron, Radisson wrote, "we entered into a strait [the St. Marys River] which had ten leagues in length [about thirty miles], full of islands where we wanted not fish. We came after to a rapid that makes the separation of the Lake of the Hurons [from] that we call Superior or Upper, for the wildmen [i.e., the Huron guides] hold it to be longer and broader [than Lake Huron] besides a great many islands which makes [it] appear in a bigger extent." Radisson knew a couple of his guides were Saulteurs and apparently expected to find a village at the falls. He saw not a soul. It seems likely that the Ojibwe had temporarily abandoned the site because of the Iroquois threat. (Radisson chased a band of Iroquois away from the falls on his return the following year.) The party did "make good cheer" of whitefish, however. Along the shore of the river[,] bear, beaver, and elk "showed themselves often, but to their [loss]."

Radisson's journal continued: "The weather was agreeable when we began to navigate upon that great extent of water. Finding it so calm, and air so clear, we thwarted [i.e., went straight across] in a pretty broad place [Whitefish Bay] and came to an isle most delightful for the diversity of its fruits." They paddled through the night before making camp at dawn. Hugging the shore the next day, they came upon a small stream that "my dearest friends" [the Indian guides] called "a small river of copper." When Radisson inquired further, the guides landed the canoes and ushered him to "a place, which is not two hundred paces in the wood[,] where many pieces of copper were uncovered. Further he told me that the mountains I saw [evidently the highlands separating Lake Superior's watershed from Lake Huron's] was of nothing else. Seeing it so fair and pure, I had a mind to take a piece of it, but they hindered me, telling my brother there was more where we were to go."

Continuing along the shore, Radisson marveled at the immense sand dunes at Au Sable Point and the "bank of rocks" that culminated in the Grand Portal, a rock arch several hundred feet high. Radisson also remarked on the many caves along the rocky shore where waves crash in and "make a most horrible noise, most like the shooting of great guns." Storms drove them ashore at Keweenaw Bay, and they sat for three

Radisson and Groseilliers hired both Huron and Ojibwe guides and paddlers for their exploration of Lake Superior. Artist Frederic Remington imagined the scene more than two centuries later. [*Radisson and Groseilliers*, 1905, Frederic Remington (1861–1909), oil on canvas, 17.125" x 30.125"; Buffalo Bill Historical Center, Cody, Wyoming; Gift of Mrs. Karl Frank; 14.86]

days waiting for fair weather to portage across Keweenaw Point. The twenty-mile crossing was made mostly by stream and beaver pond, and it saved the party from an eight-day paddle around the end of the point. Radisson noted that the portage trail "was well beaten because of the comers and goers" of Indian parties.

On the shore west of the peninsula, they came upon a village of Ojibwe. Seven canoes of Ojibwe men joined the expedition, "in hopes," Radisson thought, "to get knives from us, which they love better than we serve God, which should make us blush for shame." A day later the party came to a long sand spit (Long Island) that sheltered the waters of Chequamegon Bay. A short portage ("sixty paces") brought them to the bay, where they immediately fell to fishing, catching a "great store of fishes, sturgeons of a vast bigness and pikes of seven feet long." The Huron/Ottawa guides claimed that their home village lay five days' trek into the interior, and they invited the Frenchmen to spend the winter. The Indians departed to seek their wives for help carrying the Frenchmen's baggage, and the two brothers-in-law spent the interval building a small log fort to store most of their trading goods. Local residents turned up at the fort periodically out of curiosity, but none of them presented a threat. "We were Caesars," Radisson wrote, "being nobody to contradict us."

They spent a hard winter of hunger in the Huron/Ottawa village, but in the spring they found their cache of trading goods unmolested. After trading with the Dakota (in present-day Minnesota), the two Frenchmen completed their mission with a hazardous paddle amid spring ice floes across the western end of Lake Superior to visit the Cree. On the north shore they swapped their remaining tools and trinkets for several boat-loads of beaver pelts.

Radisson, who habitually extracted from the Indians all the geograph-ical information they had, learned from the Cree about a series of water-ways to the north of Lake Superior that led to a great salt sea. The Cree spoke of a large lake (Nipigon) that drained into Lake Superior. From its waters, they claimed, there was a portage leading to a great river (the Albany) that emptied into the salt sea, which Radisson correctly surmised was Hudson Bay. He instantly recognized the significance of this intelligence, for it promised a back door to the beaver country. A downriver trip to Hudson Bay would be easier and shorter than hauling furs all the way to Montreal; further, it would avoid Iroquois territory. Radisson would mull the idea of a trading post on Hudson Bay all the way back to Montreal.

In their winter of trading, Radisson and Groseilliers amassed enough beaver, marten, and otter pelts to fill sixty Indian canoes. They easily found volunteers to make the voyage, and the flotilla reached Montreal on August 20, 1660. The market value of their furs came to 140,000 livres—a livre was roughly equivalent to a Spanish dollar—and literally saved the floundering economy of New France. The colony's ungrateful governor nevertheless clapped Radisson and Groseilliers in jail because they were not licensed traders. The Company of New France, which had a monopoly on the fur trade, seized most of their furs.

Freed from jail, the brothers-in-law sailed to France to seek redress from the king. Receiving only empty promises, they carried to England their idea of a post on Hudson Bay. In 1668–69 Groseilliers sailed a vessel with an English crew into the bay and spent the winter at its southernmost tip, which he named James Bay. His return with a cargo of pelts worth £19,000 caught the attention of English investors, and in 1670 King Charles II signed a charter for the Hudson's Bay Company, an institution that would have a major impact on the Lake Superior fur trade. The English presence on Hudson Bay also had important strategic implications, for it set the stage for a half century of conflict that would end in the fall of New France and a change in flags over Lake Superior.

The White and Gold Fleur-de-Lis

In 1661 King Louis XIV took royal possession of New France and made the fur trade a government monopoly. Prior to that date, the government and lands of the colony had been in the hands of a private company or, rather, a succession of companies, partnerships, and cartels that had been granted rights by the crown, including a monopoly on the fur trade. After 1661 the trade was subject to royal regulations, but it remained in the hands of the merchants of Quebec and Montreal. While the Indians continued as middlemen, gradually they no longer had to travel all the way to Montreal. During the 1660s the French set up trading posts on Mackinac Island in the straits between lakes Huron and Michigan and at Chequamegon Bay. The merchants of Quebec and Montreal sent men to these posts to trade with the Indians and return with furs.

Fur traders who went west were required to obtain a license from the governor. Royal regulations limited the number of licenses issued each year and did so for three reasons: to maintain a stable price for furs, to prevent the St. Lawrence settlements from becoming depopulated, and to weed out unscrupulous traders who might cheat the Indians or sell them liquor. The licensing system proved impossible to enforce, however, and hundreds of interlopers (*coureurs de bois*), abetted by greedy merchants and army officers, plied the interior waterways, trading with the Indians.

The trader best known and loved by the Indians of the Northwest was Nicolas Perrot. Trained by the Jesuits, he had done missionary work among the Indians and learned several Algonquian tongues. In 1667 he left church service and entered into an agreement with two Montreal fur merchants. Outfitted by the merchants and holding a license from the governor, Perrot was to travel to the western lakes and collect furs from the Indians. He could keep half the furs as his compensation; the merchants took the other half. In summer 1667, Perrot accompanied a fleet of Ottawa canoes to Lake Superior and spent the winter at Chequamegon Bay. The following spring a delegation of Potawatomi from Green Bay invited him to visit their village. He did so and returned to Montreal in the fall of 1668 with a huge cargo of furs.

In 1671 the governor of New France decided to stage a pageant at Sault Ste. Marie in which his emissary would officially lay claim to the western lakes and simultaneously impress the Indians with France's grandeur. He gave Perrot the job of rounding up tribal delegates from Green Bay to Lake Winnipeg. On June 14, 1671, the personal representative of the French king, Francois Daumont St. Lusson, dressed in the uniform of a French army officer with a gleaming helmet bearing the royal fleur-de-lis, addressed the representatives of fourteen western tribes. After making formal claim to all of the continent as far as the "South Sea," St. Lusson led a parade of painted and befeathered Indians, black-robed priests singing Latin hymns, and red-sashed voyageurs (men who paddled the traders' canoes) through the village of Sault Ste. Marie. On the lake's shore, with the roar of the falls in the background, he planted a cross and near it a cedar post bearing the arms of the "most redoubtable monarch, Louis XIV, the most Christian king of France and Navarre."

The emptiness of French pretensions became apparent as the Dakota disrupted the fur trade on the south shore of Lake Superior for several years. Nicolas Perrot, ever adaptable, moved his trading post to the St. Croix River in the middle of Dakota country.

Because of the Indian warfare, the next Frenchman to venture the length of Lake Superior was neither a trader nor a missionary but a soldier, Daniel Greysolon, Sieur du Lhut (Duluth). Born in France of a noble family, Duluth at an early age had entered the King's Guard, an elite unit of aristocrats' sons. In 1674, at age thirty-eight, he left the army and moved to Canada. An uncle in Montreal was one of New France's wealthiest merchants. A combination of his uncle's patronage and his military background earned Duluth a commission from the governor

Natives and voyageurs arrive at a trading post with their cargo of furs and goods
in Dewey Albinson's charcoal drawing *Trip's End.*

to make peace in the west. He spent the winter of 1678–79 with the
Ojibwe at Sault Ste. Marie. The Dakota had chased the Huron out of
Chequamegon Bay in order to deal directly with the French, and Duluth
had no difficulty arranging a conference with them at the western end,
or "bottom," of the lake (*fond du lac*) in the spring of 1679.

The meeting site was probably the heights overlooking the St. Louis
River. After the Dakota and Ojibwe agreed to a truce, the Dakota ushered
Duluth to their central village, Isanti, on the lake the French would later
name Mille Lacs. There, on July 2, 1679, Duluth erected a standard bear-
ing the fleur-de-lis and claimed all the Dakota country for Louis XIV.
At that very moment another French explorer, Robert Cavelier, Sieur de
La Salle, was embarking on a voyage down the Illinois and Mississippi
rivers that would claim the entire Mississippi watershed—soon named
Louisiana—for the French king.

Returning to Lake Superior, Duluth arranged a meeting at Fond du Lac
with leaders of the Assiniboin tribe, whose domain lay in the northwest

lake country, home to Lake of the Woods and Lake Winnipeg. He arranged a peace between them and their Dakota neighbors and persuaded them to send a delegation to Montreal. The need to resecure allegiance with the Indians of the western lakes had been made urgent by the founding of the competitive Hudson's Bay Company and the subsequent establishment of English posts on James Bay. The Cree Indians of Lake Superior, who had shown Radisson the route, were already sending furs northward by way of Lake Nipigon and the Albany River. Duluth's mission had been that of damage control.

In 1680, the year after Duluth's peacemaking ventures, French parties (there is disagreement among annalists as to whether Duluth himself was involved) established a post on Thunder Bay, a sheltered inlet on the north shore where the Kaministiquia River flows into Lake Superior. The Cree had no doubt acquainted the French with a canoe-portage route that led westward from the headwaters of that stream into Rainy Lake and from there into waters flowing to Lake of the Woods and Lake Winnipeg. That same year the French established a post on Lake Nipigon with the dual purpose of wooing the Cree and discouraging them from sending their furs north to the English. At the height of their power in the west, the French in the course of the 1680s seized control of the English posts on James Bay, though they never managed to capture the forts on the west side of Hudson Bay at the mouths of the Nelson and Hayes rivers, the outlets for Rainy Lake, Lake of the Woods, and Lake Winnipeg.

During the 1680s the Ojibwe moved westward along the south shore of Lake Superior and occupied the abandoned Huron and Ottawa villages on Chequamegon Bay. French traders returned to the bay and sometime around 1690 erected a trading post on its shore, the first since Radisson's crude hut. They placed it on the tip of Chequamegon Point (Long Island today), a site easily defended from attack, and named it La Pointe.

From 1689 to 1697 and again from 1702 to 1713, the imperial ambitions of Louis XIV kept Europe at war, and the personal struggle between Bourbon France and Stuart England spilled over into the New World. French-armed Algonquin Indians raided towns on the New England frontier, and the English retaliated by sending the Iroquois to disrupt the western fur trade. From 1690 to 1693 not a single beaver pelt reached Montreal. In the latter year, Governor Louis de Buade Frontenac ordered

DANIEL GREYSOLON SIEUR DULHUT
AT THE HEAD OF THE LAKES — 1679

The namesake of the "Zenith City," Daniel Greysolon, Sieur du Lhut, furthered the fur trade by arranging a peace between the Dakota and Assiniboin. His arrival at the "Head of the Lakes" was painted by Francis Lee Jaques.

the soldiers at Mackinac Island to escort a convoy to Montreal, guarding the furs with enough troops to overawe the Iroquois. The resulting harvest rescued the Montreal merchants from bankruptcy and reestablished the alliance, begun by Duluth, between soldiers and fur traders.

Accompanying the flotilla on its return trip was Frontenac's agent, Pierre Le Sueur, with orders to take command at Lake Superior. Born in France and educated by Jesuits, Le Sueur had served for a time as *donne,* or assistant, in the mission at Sault Ste. Marie. Lured by the profit in fur, he became a *coureur de bois* and, in partnership with Nicolas Perrot, traveled through Dakota territory, from the Minnesota River to the St. Croix. With orders to restore the trading route across Lake Superior and bring the Dakota into alliance with the French, Le Sueur in 1693 built a fort on the southwest corner of Madeline Island in Chequamegon Bay. The fur traders moved their operation from Chequamegon Point to the island fort and carried the name La Pointe with them. Le Sueur remained in the western part of Lake Superior for two years and succeeded in cementing the Dakota-Ojibwe peace Duluth had initiated.

On the Atlantic seaboard, the war did not go well for the French because the English colonies far outweighed New France in population and wealth. With the dual purpose of limiting the supply (and maintaining the price) of furs and consolidating his military strength in the St. Lawrence settlements, the French king in 1697 ordered the western forts to be abandoned. Twenty years would pass before the French regained an official presence on Lake Superior. In the interim, the unregulated *coureurs de bois* became the middlemen in the fur trade and brandy supplemented the knives, cookware, and blankets supplied to the Indians.

In the brief interval between wars, the French in 1701 at last arranged a permanent peace with the Iroquois, whose ranks had been thinned by war and disease, and established a fort and trading post at Detroit, intending to make it the focal point of the western trade. The struggle with the English that resumed the following year again went badly for the French. In 1710 the British seized the maritime colony of Acadia, renaming it Nova Scotia, and British victories in Europe ended a half century of French military dominance on that continent. By the Peace of Utrecht in 1713, the French ceded Nova Scotia and Newfoundland to the British and abandoned any claim to Hudson Bay.

With the end of fighting, the French king reinstated the fur licensing system and offered amnesty to any illegal trader who would return to the St. Lawrence settlements. The military post on Mackinac Island was restored, and in 1717 the governor dispatched Zacharie Robutel, Sieur de la Noue, a veteran of the colonial war, to rebuild the fort at Kaministiquia (Thunder Bay). La Noue left Montreal with eight canoeloads of men and trading goods. He remained on Lake Superior for four years and made Kaministiquia the terminal for a trade route that stretched west to Lake Winnipeg.

In 1718 a French military detachment built a new fort at La Pointe on Madeline Island in Chequamegon Bay. This fort lay a quarter of a mile south of the old one on an inlet that afforded a better landing for canoes. The Ojibwe by this time had a major settlement on the shore of the

VISITING HISTORY

Radisson-Groseilliers Landing Site (Highway 2 at the western limits of Ashland, Wisconsin) is identified by a Wisconsin Historical Society marker to show where the "Caesars of the Wilderness" built a crude cabin in 1659.

Ermatinger Old Stone House (Queen Street East, Sault Ste. Marie, Ontario) was built in 1814 by a wealthy fur trader and is the oldest house in Canada west of Toronto. A self-guided tour provides insights on the fur trade business.

Madeline Island Historical Museum (near the ferry dock, Madeline Island, Wisconsin) consists of four log structures, one a historic fur warehouse, owned by the Wisconsin Historical Society. An automobile/ passenger ferry operates regularly from Bayfield to Madeline Island from April ice-out to the December freeze.

The **Northern Great Lakes Center** (Highway G, Ashland, Wisconsin) exhibit hall focuses on the history of the region, including the fur trade.

bay—today's Ashland—and villages to the east on the wild rice sloughs of Bad River and to the south at Lac Court Oreilles.

About this time, the name *Apostle Islands* began to appear on French maps. The group of islands afforded protection for the shipping in Chequamegon Bay and, except for the post at La Pointe, were uninhabited. The Indians believed them haunted because of the eerie sounds the wind and waves made in caves along the shore. It has long been assumed that they were named by Jesuits, in reference to the number of islands in the group. However, twelve of the islands are not visible from any observation point on the Bayfield Peninsula or Chequamegon Point, and, further, a person who canoes among them will count more than twelve. The name may have originated from a nest of pirates who inhabited the islands for a time, calling themselves the Twelve Apostles.

The French government expected the western posts to be more or less self-supporting; thus, officials looked the other way when army officers assigned there took along boatloads of trading goods. When Ensign Jacques Le Gardeur de St. Pierre was appointed second-in-command of the post at La Pointe in 1729, he purchased on credit four thousand livres of trade goods from a Montreal merchant (who also happened to be his brother-in-law). The bulk of the cargo was woolen cloth, which the Indians presumably made into garments, but it also included blankets, knives and axes, seventy-five *pots* of brandy (a *pot* was approximately a half gallon), and 260 pounds of tobacco. Smaller articles included two dozen sewing needles, three hundred gunflints, and a keg of gunpowder. St. Pierre also carried, presumably for his own use, two bushels of peas, 517 pounds of hardtack (crackers), 137 pounds of bacon, and thirty *pots* of wine. The commander of the post at La Pointe, Louis Denis, Sieur de la Ronde, was even more commercially ambitious. Learning from the Indians of the free copper nodes along the Ontonagon River, he made the seventy-mile journey, collected a number of specimens, and sent them to France for assay. Without waiting for the results, he began to think of transporting the ore. Carrying it by canoe was impractical, so he went to the Sault, constructed a boatyard, and in 1731 launched the first sailing vessel onto Lake Superior.

The richness of the specimens La Ronde had sent to Paris so impressed the French ministry that it sent two experienced engineers to help him

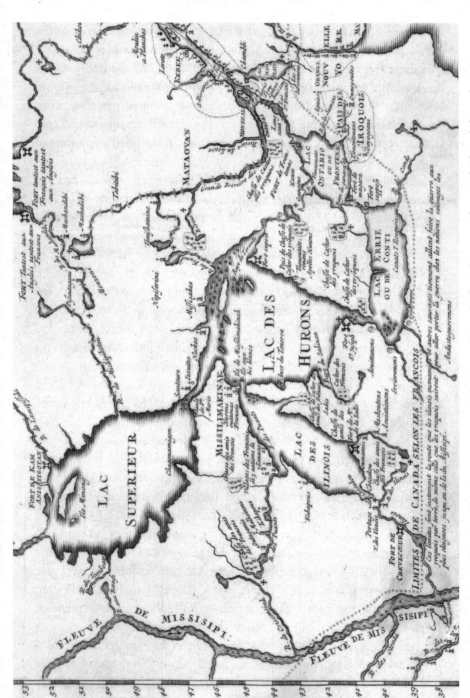

This 1719 map by Henri Chatelain features the waterways of the Great Lakes and reflects the extent of geographic knowledge at the time.

locate a mine. He opened the mine in 1732 and shipped the ore to the Sault, where it was carried around the falls and loaded onto another sailing vessel on Lake Huron. La Ronde had to abandon his mining efforts and resume his military duties when warfare broke out once again between the Ojibwe and the Dakota—a war that eventually pushed many of the Dakota people out onto the western plains. A century would pass before copper mining resumed and ore boats again plied the waters of Lake Superior.

Reestablishment of the posts on Lake Superior was not the limit of French ambitions when the European warfare ended. The Cree and Assiniboin had made the French well aware of canoe routes to the western lakes: establishing outposts there was the next logical step. La Noue had been ordered to proceed to Lake Winnipeg after he finished work on Kaministiquia, but he never did so. In 1728 Pierre Gaultier de La Verendrye became Kaministiquia's commander and listened to Indian descriptions of water routes from Lake Superior to Lake Winnipeg. Among the most interesting was an Ojibwe tale of a shorter route that began thirty miles south of Kaministiquia at the mouth of a small stream that would later be named the Pigeon River. It began with a nine-mile portage (soon called the Grand Portage) up and over the granite bluffs of the north shore; from there a succession of lakes and rivers led into Rainy Lake and an all-water route to Lake of the Woods and Lake Winnipeg.

In 1730 the governor authorized La Verendrye to establish forts in the west and gave him two thousand livres to buy presents for the Indians. To finance the expedition the governor also granted him a three-year monopoly on the furs sent back from Lake Superior. La Verendrye's fifty-man crew, which included three of his four sons, departed Montreal in June 1731. At Kaministiquia, La Verendrye sent an advance detachment, commanded by his eldest son, to explore the Grand Portage route. This party reached Rainy Lake before the snows set in and built a small fort at its northeastern end. La Verendrye joined them the following summer, and the explorers paddled out onto Lake of the Woods in September 1732. Over the next twelve years, La Verendrye and his sons built posts on Lake Winnipeg and the Saskatchewan River and explored the plains south to the Missouri River and west to the Rocky Mountains. For the Lake Superior fur trade, however, La Verendrye's great achievement was establishing the Grand Portage and verifying the quickest route to the western waters.

Despite La Verendrye's exploits, the French role in the European fur market went into decline. American Indians, experienced traders long before the Europeans appeared, preferred English woolens, particularly their tightly woven blankets, and cheap British rum. Despite the French posts at Nipigon and Winnipeg, the Ojibwe and Cree of Lake Superior carried most of their furs to the British at Hudson Bay. Other factors came into play as well, including the French strategies of giving blankets as gifts rather than in trade and of marrying natives to become part of their community.

The French hat industry—the principal user of beaver pelts—also went into decline in the eighteenth century. Louis XIV, among the many mistakes of his seventy-two-year reign, revoked the Edict of Nantes, by which the Catholic monarchy had tolerated French Protestants (Huguenots). Threatened with persecution, the Huguenots fled to the Netherlands and Germany. The city of La Rochelle on the Bay of Biscay, the hub of both Protestantism and hat making, became virtually depopulated. Hat making centers sprang up in the Netherlands and Germany, and they looked to Britain for a supply of prime beaver pelts. By the middle of the eighteenth century, the French traders at Montreal, who had never built an organization capable of competing with the Hudson's Bay Company, subsisted from year to year on diminishing profit margins.

The renewal of warfare in Europe and North America completed the demise of New France and French control of Lake Superior. In 1740 war broke out between Prussia and Austria; Britain (ally of Austria) and France (ally of Prussia) became embroiled four years later. The British navy halted all French trade with the St. Lawrence settlements, and beaver skins piled up in Montreal warehouses. A French official complained that he felt "obliged to give the Indians beaver skins instead of goods to make their clothing . . . [because] they are naked." The glut backed up all the way to Lake Superior: La Pointe in Chequamegon Bay sent eastward a mere 250 bundles of fur a year.

The war ended in 1748, but peace was only temporary. Both sides maneuvered for advantage in North America. In the east, the French began building forts on the canoe route between Lake Erie and the

A beaver colony. The beaver's pelt was the most coveted during the early years of the fur trade. Only after the beaver was mostly trapped out did traders turn to muskrat and other animals.

Allegheny (upper Ohio) River; the British countered by encouraging Virginians to cross the mountains and settle on the Ohio River. In the west, the French governor recognized the strategic importance of Sault Ste. Marie. In 1750 he instructed Chevalier de Repentigny, a soldier stationed at Michilimackinac (the Ojibwe name for Mackinac Island), to build a fort at the Sault. Repentigny, the thirty-year-old son of a wealthy Quebec merchant, was apparently expected to finance the construction himself. As reimbursement, the governor gave him a license to trade and granted him a tract of land that extended for eighteen miles along the banks of the St. Marys River. The fort, consisting of a wooden stockade enclosing three buildings, was completed in the summer of 1751. In the first attempt at agriculture on the shores of Lake Superior, Repentigny brought from Mackinac "a bull, two oxen, three cows, two heifers, a horse and a mare." Repentigny befriended Jean Baptiste Cadotte, a Frenchman living at the Sault with an Ojibwe wife variously known as Marianne or Anastasia, and gave him a small tract of land on which to plant corn. Cadotte was left in charge of the outpost when Repentigny went east in 1759 to fight the British.

The fighting had resumed in 1754 when a young Virginia militia officer, George Washington, contested French advances into the Ohio Valley; war was formally declared two years later. This time North America was the principal battleground. Again it went badly for the French: Quebec fell to the British in 1759, and the following year in Montreal the governor surrendered all of New France. By the Treaty of Paris (1763) Britain obtained possession of Canada and the part of Louisiana that lay east of the Mississippi; Spain gained French claims west of the Mississippi. British troops took over the outposts at Sault Ste. Marie, Kaministiquia, Grand Portage, and La Pointe.

An act of parliament in 1707 had joined England and Scotland into a single nation, the United Kingdom of Great Britain. Symbolizing the union was a new national flag containing the English Cross of St. George and the Scottish Cross of St. Andrew. Affectionately known as the Union Jack, it now flew over Lake Superior.

Under the Union Jack

The British conquest of Canada had little immediate effect on the Lake Superior fur trade. Montreal merchants, mostly of French ancestry but supplemented after 1760 with a handful of Scots, continued to control the trade, though the pelts now went to Britain rather than to France. The voyageurs were almost all French. The more experienced of these contracting traders spent several years in the interior west of Lake Superior, collecting furs and bringing them to a July rendezvous at Grand Portage or Mackinac Island. Less experienced voyageurs, disparagingly referred to as "pork eaters" (*mangeurs de lard*), paddled only as far as the rendezvous and returned to Montreal the same year. The label referred to the fact that their diet included weighty items such as bacon and salt pork, while those who wintered over lived Indian-style, on pemmican and wild rice.

The Montreal canoe was thirty-five to forty feet long and required a crew of eight.

By the mid-eighteenth century, the French had developed a freight canoe that made the trip up the Ottawa River and across Huron and Superior to the rendezvous points. Called the Montreal canoe, it was thirty-five to forty feet long, spanned five to six feet at the center, and weighed six hundred pounds. It was capable of carrying five tons of men and furs. Because the craft was ungainly as well as heavy, six men were required to carry it over a portage, such as around the falls at Sault Ste. Marie. To that point, it usually had a crew of fourteen: twelve paddlers plus a bowman and a steersman. On Lake Superior, only five to eight voyageurs manned the freight canoe so that it rode higher on the sometimes rough freshwater sea.

Scholar Grace Lee Nute described the rugged voyageurs as being of fairly uniform height and appearance. They stood no more than five feet six inches tall (the average height of European men of that era); employers rejected anyone taller because there was little legroom in a tightly packed canoe. They had powerful arms and shoulders because of the constant paddling and portaging. On a portage, each man carried a standard load of two ninety-pound packs of pelts. They were a color-ful band, their hair long and heavily greased as protection against mosquitoes, sporting gaily hued sashes and tobacco pipes. To maintain a paddling rhythm and relieve the tedium, they sang French *chansons*. A favorite recorded by travelers was *"Voici le Printemps"* ("In the Gay Spring Time"):

> Voici le printemps, les amours se renouvellent,
> Et tous les amants vont changer de maitresse.
> Le bon vin m'endort, l'amour m'y réveille.
> Changera qui voudra, moi je garde la mienne.
> Elle a les yeux doux, et la bouche vermeille.
> Le bon vin m'endort, l'amour m'y reveille.
>
> [See the spring is here,
> Our loves we are a-waking,
> And lovers all now
> New mistresses are taking.
> Good old wine makes me doze,
> But love keeps me a-waking.
> Let all those change who may,
> I keep to my old mistress.
> So soft are her eyes
> And so tender are her kisses.
> Good old wine makes me doze,
> But love keeps me a-waking.]

A traveler of the early nineteenth century, Thomas McKenney, re-corded the amazing stamina of the voyageurs. They paddled from dawn to dusk, which made for very long days in a northern summer. Concerned for the welfare of his paddlers, McKenney asked them at seven o'clock one evening if they were ready to go ashore for the night. "They answered," he related in his journal, "they were fresh yet. They had been almost constantly paddling since 3 o'clock this morning . . . 57,600 strokes with the paddle, and 'fresh yet'! No human beings, except the Canadian French, could stand this. Encamped . . . at half past nine o'clock, having come today *seventy-nine miles*." His figure of 57,600 was based on a timed estimate of fifty strokes a minute.

While on the lake the voyageurs ate two virtually identical meals a day—when they arose in the morning and when they retired at night. A company clerk on his way to the post at Grand Portage described the food preparation:

> The tin kettle, in which they cooked their food, would hold eight or ten gallons. It was hung over the fire [at night], nearly full of water, then nine quarts of [dried] peas—one quart per man, the daily allowance—were put in; and when they were well bursted, two or three pounds of pork, cut into strips, for seasoning, were added, and all allowed to boil or simmer till daylight, when the cook added four biscuits, broken up, to the mess, and invited all hands to breakfast. The swelling of the peas and biscuit had now filled the kettle to the brim, so thick that a stick would stand upright in it. It looked inviting, and I begged for a plate full of it, and ate little else during the journey. The men now squatted in a circle, the kettle in their midst, and each one plying his wooden spoon or ladle from kettle to mouth, with almost electric speed, soon filled every cavity. Then the pipes were brought out into full smoke.

The clerk—probably a young son of a Montreal merchant—seemed uncomplaining, but other travelers were more critical. One journalist claimed that the difficulty of persuading "any other men than Canadians, to [dine on] this fare, seems to secure to them . . . the monopoly of the fur trade."

The Montreal canoes were so fragile that tent poles were placed on the bottom to equalize the cargo's weight. Every canoe carried a giant sponge, capable of soaking up a pailful at a time, to handle the water that leaked through the seams or lapped over the gunwale. Every night the canoes were turned over on the shore, and any damaged seams were resealed with hot pitch. Landing a loaded canoe was tricky because it was too fragile to be run up on a beach. One journalist described the landing of a brigade of Montreal canoes at Grand Portage: "The first [canoe] makes a dash at the beach. Just as the last wave is carrying the canoe on dry ground, all her men jump out at once and support her; while her gentlemen or clerks hurry out her lading. During this time the other canoes are, if possible, heading out into the lake; but now one approaches, and is seized by the crew of the canoe first beached, who meet her up to the middle in water, and who, assisted by her own people [unload the cargo and] lift her up high and dry." Six men then carried the canoe gently onto the shore.

One of the first English traders (actually an American, born in New Jersey) to arrive on the shores of Lake Superior when the fighting ended was Alexander Henry. Twenty-two years old, Henry left Montreal

Voyageur with Pipe, C. S. Reinhart. Voyageurs measured distance by "pipes," or breaks allowed for smoking and storytelling.

in the summer of 1761 with a load of trade goods bound for Fort Michilimackinac. The following spring he made the four-day canoe paddle to Sault Ste. Marie. He described the place in his journal: "There is at present a village of Chippeways [Ojibwe], of fifty warriors, seated at this place; but the inhabitants reside here during the summer only, going westward in the winter to hunt. The village was anciently much more populous."

The only Frenchman at the Sault was Jean Baptiste Cadotte, who lived in the fort with his Ojibwe wife and family. Henry wrote, "In the family of M. Cadotte no other language than the Chippeway was spoken." Eager to learn the language, Henry spent the summer and fall with the Cadottes. He returned to Michilimackinac, narrowly missed being killed when Ottawa Indians massacred the garrison there as part of the Pontiac Conspiracy of 1763, and spent the next two years living among the Ojibwe.

Returning to Montreal, he badgered the British military governor for a trade concession in the west. He apparently made such a nuisance of himself that the governor, hoping to be rid of him, granted a three-year monopoly of the Lake Superior fur trade. At Michilimackinac he purchased on twelve months' credit food (fifty bushels of corn) and enough trade goods to fill four Montreal canoes. Proceeding to Sault Ste. Marie, he formed a partnership with Cadotte, who apparently had helped finance the purchase of the trade goods, and moved on to Chequamegon Bay. At La Pointe on Madeline Island, he built a trading post a short distance from the old French fort. By the spring of 1766 he had disposed of all his trade goods, collecting 150 packs of beaver and twenty-five packs of otter and martin skins, each pack weighing ninety pounds. Harold A. Innis, premier historian of the Canadian fur trade, summarized, "The success of the partnership of Henry and Cadotte was symbolic of the necessary combination between English capital and French experience."

The partnership continued for more than a decade, and their operations extended into the waterways beyond the Grand Portage. The outbreak of the American Revolution in 1775 had little effect on the Lake Superior fur trade. Alexander Henry may have been the only American-born trader in the region, and he maintained correct relations with his backers in Montreal. To ensure the loyalty, or at least the neutrality, of the French traders, the governor of Canada sent a contingent of British-Canadian soldiers to the Grand Portage in 1778. The officer commanding the expedition reported some political disaffection among the voyageurs but otherwise business as usual. Some forty thousand pounds of furs passed through the settlement annually, he wrote, and the trade involved about five hundred individuals who, "for about a month in the summer season, have a general rendezvous at the Portage, and for the refreshing and comforting [of] those who are employed in the more distant voyages the Traders from hence [Montreal] have built tolerable Houses; and in order to cover them [i.e., the trading goods] from any insult from the numerous savage Tribes, who resort there during that time, have made stockades around them."

Although the United States gained its independence by the peace treaty of 1783, with a northern boundary drawn through the middle of the Great Lakes and a western boundary at the Mississippi River, British traders in Montreal and French voyageurs continued to dominate the Lake Superior trade. However, the British merchants recognized the need for better organization. As early as 1775, Alexander Henry reported that traders at Grand Portage were "in a state of extreme reciprocal hostility, each pursuing his interests in such a manner as might most injure his neighbour. The consequences were very hurtful to the morals of the Indians."

That same year a consortium of Montreal merchants sent a huge shipment of trade goods west with seventy-five men in twelve canoes. This marked the beginning of a series of combinations and limited partnerships among Montreal merchants that culminated in the formation of the North West Company in the mid-1780s. Although the new company issued shares like a modern corporation, it was essentially an alliance of independent mercantile houses. Each kept separate books and dealt in furs in proportion to the number of shares it owned. In 1787 Alexander Henry and Jean Baptiste Cadotte sold their partnership interests and the post at Chequamegon Bay to the North West Company and retired, Henry to Montreal and Cadotte to Sault Ste. Marie, where his descendents today make up a sizable portion of the population.

The advantages of corporate organization were soon evident. To improve upon the speed and carrying capacity of the Montreal canoes, the company purchased a sailing vessel, which made four or five trips each summer between Sault Ste. Marie and Grand Portage. On the landing at Grand Portage, the company built a new stockade of more than a hundred yards on each side. Inside, wrote one visitor, were sixteen buildings "made with cedar and white spruce fir split with whipsaws after being squared" and "painted with Spanish brown." Six of the buildings were storehouses, and the remainder included a counting house, residences, and a mess hall that could feed one hundred men at a time. By 1800 the settlement at Grand Portage possessed a herd of cattle and a vegetable garden of several acres.

The settlement at Sault Ste. Marie experienced a similar revival. In 1789 the explorer Alexander Mackenzie wrote disparagingly of the village at the foot of the falls as "formerly a place of great resort for the inhabitants of Lake Superior, and consequently of considerable trade: it is now, however, dwindled to nothing, and reduced to about thirty families, of the Algonquin nation, who are one half of the year starving, and the other half intoxicated, and ten or twelve Canadians, who have been in the Indian country from an early period of life, and intermarried with the natives." In 1797 the North West Company built a three-thousand-foot canal on the Canadian side of the falls with a lock that could raise the water nine feet. The canal accommodated only canoes, however, because it was only two feet deep and had a strong current. By 1800 the company had three sailing vessels plying the lake between the Sault and Grand Portage. Its sailors had dragged the ships on rollers around the falls. By that date also the North West Company was constructing a sawmill at the foot of the rapids to furnish boards for construction both locally and at Grand Portage.

Two Flags over the Lake

For a decade after the end of the Revolution, the American government was too weak to impose its authority on the Lake Superior region. Exploiting the situation, the British maintained military posts on American soil in violation of the peace treaty. The most important of these were at Detroit and Michilimackinac. They also had a small garrison at Grand Portage, but it was not clear whether this post was on American soil. The peace

At Grand Portage, or the "Great Carrying Place," the North West Company's post hosted traders from Montreal and voyageurs who had paddled the interior to secure furs. Today, reconstructed buildings offer a window into the site's history.

treaty of 1783 had drawn the American-Canadian boundary through the middle of Lake Superior and the western boundary of the United States at the Mississippi River, but it left a gap between Lake Superior and the still-unknown source of the Mississippi. By the Jay Treaty of 1794, the British agreed to evacuate the North West posts, and they did so two years later. They even withdrew their troops from Grand Portage.

Prior to 1796, American fur traders, the most prominent of whom was John Jacob Astor, had confined their trade to the region south and west of Lake Superior. In the late 1790s, benefiting from a law that imposed heavy import duties on trade goods coming from British Canada into the United States, they moved aggressively into Lake Superior. The North West Company traders in Montreal became concerned for the future of Grand Portage, should that outpost ultimately be found to reside on American soil. In 1798 a Scot explorer rediscovered the old French trading route from Thunder Bay inland by way of the Kaministiquia River (spelled *Kaministikwia* by the British). Although this route to Rainy Lake and Lake of the Woods was longer than that from Grand Portage, it clearly lay on the Canadian side of the border.

In 1802 the North West Company began constructing an outpost at the mouth of the Kaministiquia River, naming it Fort William, after company director William McGillivray. Well before the fort was completed in 1811, the company had moved its annual rendezvous to Thunder Bay. The fort was by far the largest structure yet built on Lake Superior. It had a palisade fifteen feet high. Inside, wrote one visitor, were enough buildings to give it "the appearance of a charming village." On the west side of the stockade, wrote another traveler, "there is a range of buildings . . . one for dressing out the employees, one for putting out the canoes, one in which merchandize is retailed, another where strong drink, bread, lard, butter, etc. are sold, and where refreshments are given

 **VISITING HISTORY**

Grand Portage National Monument (Grand Portage, Minnesota) contains a replica of the North West Company's fur trade post. The 8.5-mile Grand Portage Trail, maintained by the National Park Service, provides spectacular views of the falls of the Pigeon River.

Fort William Historical Park (off Highway 61, Thunder Bay, Ontario) contains a reconstruction of the North West Company's Fort William, with an interpretive outdoor museum on the banks of the Kaministiquia River.

The American Fur Company ran trading posts including the one at Fond du Lac, shown here in a sketch from 1827.

out to arriving voyageurs." Each canoeist was allowed on arrival a loaf of bread, a half pound of butter, and a quart of rum. Those who consumed the rum all at once were carted off to jail to spend the night, many with half a pound of butter still in hand. The jail was appropriately named the Butter Tub.

In 1808 John Jacob Astor incorporated his business under the laws of New York as the American Fur Company. He was not, however, able to break the British stranglehold on the Lake Superior trade until after the War of 1812, when Congress passed an act excluding foreigners from engaging in the fur trade on American territory. In 1816–17 Astor's American Fur Company purchased, at a rock-bottom price, the North West Company's trading posts at Sault Ste. Marie and La Pointe. Sometime thereafter it rebuilt the post at Grand Portage.

In 1821 the North West Company was absorbed by the Hudson's Bay Company. Western furs thereafter went to the northern sea, the Kaministiquia route was abandoned, and Fort William fell into disuse. By the 1820s the supply of beaver in the streams around Lake Superior was virtually exhausted, and the locus of the American fur trade shifted to the Rocky Mountains. By 1822, when the U.S. Army finally erected a fort at Sault Ste. Marie, the trading post there was shipping more fish than furs to the East Coast. The same was true at La Pointe in Chequamegon Bay. In 1833 Astor's American Fur Company signed a secret agreement with the Hudson's Bay Company by which the British company paid the Americans three hundred pounds a year to cease fur operations in the Lake Superior region. Thereafter, the once-glorious post at Grand Portage became a fishing station. The era of the fur trade on the lake was at an end.

Jane Johnston Schoolcraft, a native of Sault Ste. Marie who was of Ojibwe and Irish descent, later wrote of U.S. advancement at the Sault:

> Adieu, to days of homebred ease,
> When many a rural care could please,
> We trim our sail anew, to steer
> By shoals we never knew were here,
> And with the star flag, raised on high
> Discover a new dominion nigh,
> And half in joy, half in fear,
> Welcome the proud Republic here.

CHAPTER FOUR

PATH OF THE PADDLE AND OAR

ALTHOUGH THE Territory of Michigan had been created in 1805, it was Indian country until the War of 1812. The only white habitations were Detroit, Michilimackinac, and Sault Ste. Marie, each thinly populated by retired voyageurs and their Indian wives. In 1813, following General William Henry Harrison's victory over the British and their Indian allies at the Battle of the Thames, President James Madison named Lewis Cass, an Ohio attorney who had been one of Harrison's lieutenants, governor of the Michigan Territory. Cass spent the next twenty years advertising and developing Michigan and its Great Lakes shoreline. In 1817 he persuaded newly elected president James Monroe to add Detroit to his tour of the nation, and, with the president's support, in 1818 he extinguished the Indian title to southern Michigan and put up the lands for public sale. That same year Illinois became a state, and the lands to its north—present-day Wisconsin and Minnesota east of the Mississippi River—were added to Michigan Territory.

In 1819 Cass wrote to Monroe's secretary of war, John C. Calhoun, recommending that he establish a military garrison at Sault Ste. Marie and suggesting that the War Department finance an exploring party to examine the south shore of Lake Superior and the possibility of a canoe route between the western end of the lake and the Mississippi River. Such an expedition, he argued, would secure allegiance from the Indian tribes along the lake, obtain land at Sault Ste. Marie for the military post, investigate the potential for copper mining, and ascertain the condition of the British fur trade on Lake Superior. A British-American convention in 1818 had agreed on an American-Canadian boundary that would follow the main channel of the St. Marys River and divide Lake Superior evenly. Both countries were establishing commissions to chart the exact boundary. Governor Cass wanted to ensure a firm hold on whatever portion of the lake fell on the American side.

Scientific Exploration of the South Shore

Secretary Calhoun, a man of extraordinary vision before he became absorbed with the provincial fears of his native South Carolina, readily approved the expedition and authorized a thousand dollars for the purpose. He also ordered Cass to take along a "topographical engineer" (a mapmaker) and "a person acquainted with zoology, botany, and mineralogy." Cass employed army captain David B. Douglass to do the topographical work, and Calhoun himself added Henry R. Schoolcraft to the expedition as geologist and mineralogist. Schoolcraft was a self-trained scientist and failed businessman who had visited the lead mines of Missouri and published an account of his tour. He brought himself to Calhoun's attention by sending copies of his book to everyone of importance in Washington in hopes that someone would "throw something his way." Both Douglass and Schoolcraft kept diaries of the expedition that departed from Detroit in May 1820 in three birch-bark canoes. Including voyageurs, soldiers, and Indian guides, the party numbered about forty.

A traveler who ventured across Lake Superior a few years later described how the voyageurs packed a passenger-carrying Montreal canoe:

> On the bottom were laid setting-poles and a spare paddle or two (to prevent the inexperienced from putting their boot-heels through the birchbark) and over these, in the after part, a tent was folded. This formed the quarter-deck for the *bourgeois* (as they called us), and across it was laid the bedding, which had previously been made up into bolster-like packages . . . These bolsters served for our seats, and around them were disposed other articles of a soft nature, to form backs or even pillows to our sitting couches. The rest of the luggage was skillfully

distributed in other parts of the canoe, leaving room for the oarsmen to sit on boards suspended by cords from the gunnel, and a place in the stern for the steersman. The cooking utensils were usually disposed in the bow, with a box of gum for mending the canoe and a roll or two of bark by way of ship timber.

The expedition paused at Michilimackinac to pick up another canoe-load of soldiers (presumably to give Cass greater leverage in negotiating with the Indians at the Sault) and reached the St. Marys River on June 14. The village of Sault Ste. Marie was located on a grassy meadow about a half mile above the rapids. It consisted of fifteen or twenty buildings, a mixture of American Fur Company warehouses and dwellings for a half dozen French and English families. Next to it was an Ojibwe village of about two hundred people. Across the river was the fur trading store and sawmill of the North West Company.

Secretary Calhoun had approved the erection of a fort at Sault Ste. Marie both as a defense against British attack and as a strategic point from which government agents could keep watch on the Indians and regulate the trade coming off the lake. Governor Cass found that getting the secretary's approval was somewhat easier than obtaining the Indian cession of land for the post.

The Indians resisted the land sale—whether they objected to a military garrison in their midst or whether they were seeking a better price is not clear. They removed the women and children from their village, and a band of seventy or eighty armed men gathered on a hillock a few hundred yards from Cass's encampment. Ojibwe leaders met with Cass and engaged in stormy debate, after which they angrily kicked away the gifts he had set out and returned to their village. When the fiercest of the Indian leaders raised a British flag in the village, Cass was forced to act. He mustered his sixty-six soldiers, marched into the Indian village, and tore down the flag, warning the Indians that only the American flag could fly over American soil. Late in the day, some of the older Ojibwe men offered to negotiate, and a treaty was quickly signed. The Indians ceded to the United States a tract of land extending for four miles along the river above and below the falls and another four miles inland, thereby including the village of Sault Ste. Marie. The Indians reserved the right to fish in the river and received as payment a stock of blankets, knives, cookware, and broadcloth.

For the remainder of June 1820, the expedition paddled along the lake's south shore. Both Schoolcraft and Douglass provide a far more detailed description of the shoreline than any earlier traveler. They marveled at the Grand Sable, "a lofty ridge of naked sand extending nine miles along the shore, and presenting a steep acclivity towards the lake." The barrenness of the hill, on the other hand, with its sparse vegetation half-buried in the shifting sands, Schoolcraft wrote, "leave upon the mind a strong impression of bleakness and desolation." A few miles beyond the Grand Sable were the Pictured Rocks, a 150-foot cliff that extended for thirteen miles along the lake. The rocks were composed of graywacke, a dark gray sandstone, with veins of minerals running through them. Douglass explained that the Pictured Rocks got their name from the metallic ores that filled the fissures and colored them red, yellow, orange, and blue. "[W]e were struck with their picturesque beauty," he wrote, "stratified as they were, resembling more the crumbling ruins of some immense building—some huge castle wall—than the works of nature."

Douglass and Schoolcraft also offer the first detailed sketch of the portage across the Keweenaw Peninsula. It began with the ascent of a fifty-foot-wide stream, now named the Portage River. After paddling upstream for six miles, the party entered a lake that wound another twelve miles into the peninsula's interior. At the head of the lake they paddled into a small stream, barely wide enough to accommodate a canoe, and ascended another six miles. The stream was overhung with alders and clogged with fallen trees and ended in a bog where the canoes had to be dragged through the mud. The muddy trail at this point was sculpted by the centuries-old passage of Indians and fur traders. The final carrying place was a mere two thousand yards ("two Pauses") through a wetlands and pine forest to the gravelly shore of Superior.

At the mouth of the Ontonagon River the expedition camped and unloaded the canoes for a side trip to the copper rock that had been part of Lake Superior lore since the days of Radisson and Groseilliers. The exploring party proceeded up the river about twelve miles by canoe when a series of rapids halted further navigation. Indian guides then led them overland around rapids and falls for another fifteen miles across

Henry Inman's sketch of Pictured Rocks, published in Henry Schoolcraft's
Narrative Journal of Travels, show a forbidding and breathtaking landscape
that remains protected and wild today.

steep hills and through dense woods. Both Douglass and Schoolcraft
were disappointed with the rock, which failed to live up to its legend. It
measured about three and a half feet on each side and, though almost
pure copper, was much weathered and gouged by souvenir hunters. The
party had nevertheless passed a number of Indian copper mines on their
trek, and Cass's later report to Calhoun as well as a published article by
Schoolcraft helped to stimulate the copper boom of the 1840s.

Their encampment at the mouth of the Ontonagon River was near an
Ojibwe village, and the Indians offered to entertain the explorers with
dancing. The dancers' dress, as described by Douglass, reflected the meeting of cultures. Some of the men wore deerskin leggings, decorated with
shells of wampum; others wore only breechcloths (the temperature that
day had reached ninety degrees) and painted their legs with red and black
circles. Their faces were blackened with vermilion stripes on foreheads
and cheeks. Several of the men wore shirts given to them by Governor
Cass. The women, who did not dance, wore deerskin leggings and "a
sort of cloth kilt reaching a little below the knee." They draped shawls
over their upper bodies. Music introduced the dancing, wrote Douglass:

"Mass of Native Copper on the Ontonagon River" appeared with Schoolcraft's journal and illustrates difficulties faced in reaching the boulder.

The orchestra consisted of two elderly Indians, one of whom beat on a rude dull sort of tambourine while the other shook a large rattle—both accompanying with a solemn monotonous chant whose measured cadence was all about it that could be esteemed musical . . . An Indian who had a profusion of feathers on his head took his pipe-stem in one hand and a rattle in the other and began beating the earth with his feet to the measure of the music, shaking his rattle and accompanying the whole with a violent muscular exertion of his whole body. Sometimes he would merely jump up and down in this way. At others he would dance forward towards some of our company as if intending to terrify them by the hideousness of his grimaces or his threatening attitude . . . As soon as one dancer had tired himself in this way he laid the rattle and pipe-stem down at the foot of some other who immediately got up and took his place.

Curiously, Schoolcraft made no mention in his diary of this evening of dancing. Perhaps he was exhausted by the hot trek to the copper rock and spent the evening abed. Despite this lapse, he began to take an interest in Indian cultures during the course of the expedition, and he would study them for the rest of his life.

The expedition passed quickly through Chequamegon Bay, stopping only to camp on the shore opposite Madeline Island. Michael Cadotte, the American Fur Company agent at La Pointe, was at Michilimackinac on business, but the Ojibwe in the vicinity entertained—and frustrated— the explorers with tales of silver mines at undisclosed locations in the woods. The party pressed onward, and on the fifth of July paddled into the mouth of the St. Louis River, eighteen days and 490 miles from Sault Ste. Marie.

The Cass expedition went on to explore the river and portage route to the Mississippi, and it raised enough questions that a decade later the governor would undertake to find the source of that mighty river. The main aftermath of the 1820 expedition in regards to Lake Superior was its effect on the life and writings of Henry R. Schoolcraft. In 1822 Governor Cass placed him in charge of the Indian Agency at the newly erected post in Sault Ste. Marie, and shortly thereafter Schoolcraft married Jane Johnston, daughter of the American Fur Company agent John Johnston and his Ojibwe wife—herself the daughter of an important figure in the tribe.

The life of an agent was a difficult one, for he was the intermediary between a distant government and the clever yet naive natives. Schoolcraft distributed rations of bacon, beans, and tobacco and made friends of the leaders with gifts of axes, traps, and kettles. The Indians depended on him for food during unusually harsh winters and often came to him to resolve their disputes. Schoolcraft eventually set aside the Sabbath as a time of privacy for himself and his family, and he firmly refused to see any intoxicated Indian, declaring, "the President has sent me to speak to *sober* men only." Schoolcraft remained at the Sault until 1831, when he and his agency were transferred to Mackinac Island.

Aided by his father-in-law and his wife's grandfather, Schoolcraft began collecting information on the Indian tribes of the western Great Lakes. He is the first to record with scientific precision the Indians' economy, beliefs, vocabulary, and legends. His writings on Indian culture, published over the next forty years, remain American classics. In 1839 he published *Algic Researches, Comprising Inquiries Respecting the Mental Characteristics of the North American Indians,* a work that inspired Henry Wadsworth Longfellow's epic poem, *Song of Hiawatha.* Longfellow's line, "By the shore of Gitche Gumee / By the shining Big-Sea-Water," indelibly imprinted a vision of Lake Superior on the

American mind. Schoolcraft's lifework culminated in a social science landmark, *Historical and Statistical Information Respecting the History, Condition, and Prospects of the Indian Tribes of the United States,* published in six massive volumes by the Bureau of Indian Affairs.

Charting the Blue Water Highway

The treaty that had ended the American Revolution in 1783 provided that the Great Lakes would serve as the boundary between the American republic and British Canada, but British fortifications on American territory and Indian warfare prevented a precise survey of the border until after the War of 1812. The Treaty of Ghent, signed in 1814, provided for a joint British-American commission to delineate the border from Maine/New Brunswick in the east to Lake of the Woods in the west. A British-American convention in 1818 established the international boundary at the forty-ninth parallel of latitude west from Lake of the Woods to the Continental Divide.

The commissioners got started in 1816, moved slowly from Maine to Lake Ontario's outlet into the St. Lawrence River, and then rapidly divvied up the lower Great Lakes. The guiding principle was that the boundary in the lakes would be a straight line that, on average, was equidistant from the Canadian and American shores. In the rivers (Niagara, Detroit, and St. Marys), the boundary followed the main channel. In addition to determining the international boundary, the commissioners undertook to chart the lakes, mapping the shorelines and sounding the depths. This latter task fell to an English naval lieutenant, Henry Wolsey Bayfield, a veteran of both the Napoleonic Wars and the War of 1812.

Bayfield used a compass, a sextant, and a chronometer in his survey. The compass provided direction, and the sextant, which measured the angle between the horizon and the sun at noon (or the North Star at midnight), gave him the latitude, or distance north of the equator. The chronometer measured longitude: the distance east or west of the Royal Observatory at Greenwich, England. (The English arbitrarily assigned Greenwich to mark the line of zero degrees longitude shortly after the observatory was built by King Charles II, but Greenwich was not internationally recognized until 1884.)

Longitude is most easily understood as a function of time. Since the earth rotates 360 degrees every twenty-four hours, it turns fifteen degrees every hour. A degree of longitude is sixty nautical miles (sixty-eight geographical miles) at the equator, and its length fades to zero at the North Pole. Determining one's longitude was thus a simple matter of comparing the local time with that at the prime meridian, Greenwich. If, for instance, a navigator determined that the sun was at high noon at his particular location and the chronometer recording Greenwich Mean Time said one o'clock, he knew he was fifteen degrees west of Greenwich, and a table would tell him the number of miles in a degree at his particular latitude (about twenty-five nautical miles at the latitude of Lake Superior).

The trick was developing a timepiece, or chronometer, that could maintain Greenwich time with near-perfect accuracy amidst the pitch and roll of a ship and temperatures that varied with latitude. Phillip II of Spain, Louis XIV of France, and the English parliament (in 1714) offered prizes for a method and instrument that could accurately establish longitude. Finally, in 1759 an Englishman, John Harrison, invented a successful marine timekeeper. Lieutenant Bayfield used a copy of Harrison's chronometer to survey the Great Lakes. While the compass and sextant were small handheld instruments that could be carried in a canoe, the chronometer required a full-rigged sailing ship because of its size and weight. It contained numerous weights and levers to counteract a ship's pitching and rolling, and its springs were made of paired metals that responded differently to temperature change and thus compensated for variations in the weather.

By 1822 Bayfield had completed the charting of Lake Huron, and he prepared to tackle Lake Superior the following spring. At Sault Ste. Marie the British government provided him with a schooner, the *Recovery*, chartered from the Hudson's Bay Company. Bayfield had learned in earlier surveys, however, that he could map the shoreline more quickly using *bateaux*, flat-bottomed boats up to forty feet long propelled by oars. Bayfield accordingly used the *Recovery* merely to carry provisions across the lake to Fort William and for "occasionally making runs with the Chronometer."

Unfortunately, Bayfield did not keep a daily journal of his explorations. His contributions are advertised only by his end product, a chart of the lake accurate enough to guide mariners for the rest of the century. There were, however, two diarists on the expedition: Dr. John J. Bigsby, a member of the British commission, and Major Joseph Delafield, head agent of the American commission. Both men went by canoe in separate parties along the Canadian shore during the summer of 1823 from Sault Ste. Marie to Grand Portage. The Treaty of Ghent specified that the international boundary should extend northwest from Sault Ste. Marie through the center of the lake to a point equidistant between Thunder Peak and Isle Royale, where it would turn southwest to meet the shore at an as-yet undetermined point. Bigsby and Delafield apparently left the drawing of that line to Bayfield; they hugged the shore in their canoes.

Henry Bayfield used a chronometer in his survey of the Great Lakes. This modern example was worn as a wristwatch.

Both men were self-trained in scientific knowledge. Delafield referred to Bigsby as "doctor," but there is no indication where he earned that title. Bigsby's journal reveals some knowledge of geology as well as of plants and animals (the appendix to his two-volume work contains an impressive list of Canadian insects). Delafield, who was trained in law and became a professional soldier during the War of 1812, gives only a descriptive travelogue. Between them, however, they provide the first detailed description of the lake's north shore.

Bigsby's group, consisting of "the astronomer to the Boundary Commission and his party of surveyors," departed Sault Ste. Marie on June 10, 1823. Bayfield sailed in the *Recovery* June 22, and Delafield put his boats in the water the next day. The American party consisted of Delafield, "a principal surveyor," and the surveyor's assistant. The threesome traveled by canoe with a crew of six "Canadians." Their provisions and camping equipment apparently went by bateau, rowed by "a few batteau-men." Delafield carried a compass but made no mention of any other mapping equipment.

Both diarists found the north shore to be steep, rocky, and forbidding, with few inlets to shelter them from the ever present west wind. Delafield described a typical campsite as being "on a rocky shore . . . on the skirt of a wood [where] . . . the view is everywhere bounded by mountains." At Michipicoten Bay, about one hundred miles north of the Sault, Bigsby stopped at a Hudson's Bay Company outpost. The river that flowed into the bay at that point formed part of an interior canoe route that led to the company's Moose Factory on James Bay. The company agent dined with the surveying party, where they were served fresh milk, a relief after their dried-food diet. Bigsby purported to enjoy it although the cows were fed fish as a supplement to the area's meager grass. On the north shore of the bay the Bigsby party passed an immense tract of burned-over pine barrens. In conversation with an Indian family fishing along the shore, he learned that they burned the woods in order to encourage the growth of berry bushes. Blueberries and blackberries were a main staple of their diet in late summer.

At Pic Island, which lay near the northernmost point of the lake, Bigsby encountered Lieutenant Bayfield and his schooner. Bigsby wrote laconically of the encounter: "We exchanged news and civilities for a few moments, and passed on." Bayfield had left the Sault only a day or so earlier and no doubt had little to report on his mapmaking. At Pic Island Bigsby pointed his canoe due west, and in the following days passed three great bays. The first was Nipigon Bay, which on its northwest shore hosts the Nipigon River, a ninety-mile stream that descends from Lake Nipigon, at one time a key fur-trading route to Hudson Bay. Bigsby made a circuit of the bay, marveling at the crystalline water that revealed a "floor" of red granite. "The region around Nipigon Bay is full of enchanting scenery," he wrote. "As we journey up this great water we have the ever-changing pictures presented by the belt of islands on our left; while on our right we have the Nipigon mainland, an assemblage of bold mountains from 900 to 1200 feet high . . . The bay is a beautiful lake of itself, so transparent that we can, for miles together, see its red pavement, and living and dead things there inhabiting."

Bigsby hurried across the mouth of the next inlet, Black Bay, aiming his canoe at Thunder Mountain, a magnificent headland that separated Black Bay from Thunder Bay. Rounding the point, he paddled across Thunder Bay to Fort William, arriving at the decaying trading post on the last day of June. Delafield, progressing more slowly because of his bateaux, reached the fort on the sixth of July. He noted Bayfield's *Recovery* lying off the mouth of the Kaministiquia River. The American officer made no mention of any social exchange with the British party.

Neither the British nor the American commissioners could chart the international boundary west of Isle Royale because the two governments could not agree on a beginning point for the boundary between Lake Superior and Lake of the Woods. The 1783 treaty referred vaguely to a line that followed the major fur-trading route into the interior (by implication starting at Grand Portage), but it also stated that the trading route began at Long Lake. John Mitchell's 1755 map of North America, upon which Benjamin Franklin and other peace commissioners drew the boundaries of the newborn republic, contained a "Long Lake" at the mouth of the Pigeon River, but no such lake actually existed in 1783, nor has it been found in the time since.

By 1823 the British and American fur companies, with some support from enterprising officials in the two governments, were seeking to turn the ambiguity to advantage. Americans contended that the fur-trading

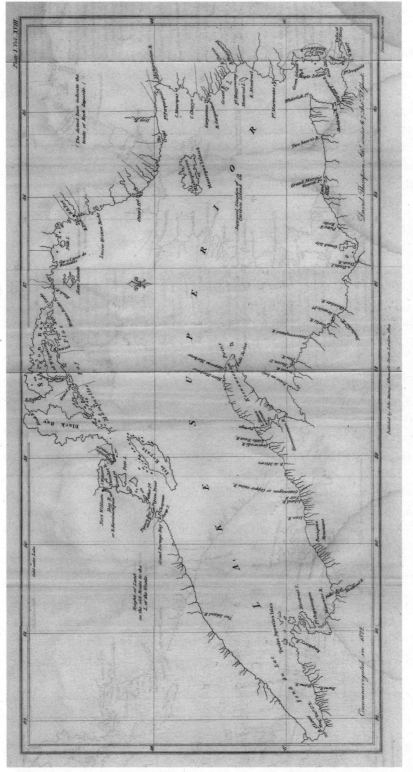

James Basire's map of Lake Superior—including tributary rivers as well as detailed notations of islands and "rock deposits"—was published with John Bigsby's notes in 1824.

route described by the 1783 treaty referred to the portage route that began at the Kaministiquia River in Thunder Bay. Some British officials
claimed instead that the imagined route began at Fond du Lac (Duluth)
and followed the St. Louis River into the interior. Caught in this cross-
fire, the British and American exploring parties in July 1823 compro-
mised on the Grand Portage route. Traveling a week apart from one
another, Bigsby and Delafield followed the old route of the voyageurs
through Rainy Lake to the Lake of the Woods. Both returned by the

VISITING HISTORY

The awesome **Pictured Rocks/Au Sable Point** (municipal dock, Munising,
Michigan) stretch of Lake Superior shoreline is visible via boat trips that
run regularly from mid-May to early October. Road trips through the park's
interior can be made from Grand Marais via Highway 77 and County
Road H58, or from Munising via Highway 28 and County Road H58.

Ontonagon County Historical Museum (River Street, Ontonagon,
Michigan) displays a replica of the Ontonagon Boulder. The Victoria
Dam Road off U.S. 45, leading to the Victoria Copper Mine, provides
good vistas of the backbreaking portages involved in hauling the boulder down to Lake Superior.

Michipicoten Island Provincial Park (nine miles from the Ontario shore
on the eastern end of the lake) is a Natural Environment Park, accessible
only by water and without developed camping sites. Tour groups depart
Michipicoten Harbor by special arrangement. A herd of caribou is one
of the island's special features.

At **Nipigon Bay/Ruby Lake Provincial Park** (Highway 17 from Nipigon
to Rossport, Ontario), the highway cuts through high cliffs of the
Laurentian Shield's red granitic rock and provides views of the fifty-six
islands in Nipigon Bay. Ruby Lake is a Natural Environment Park, still
in the planning stage, at the mouth of the Nipigon River.

Hudson's Bay Company's more northerly route to Fort William. Not until the signing of the Webster-Ashburton Treaty in 1842 did the two governments finally settle on the Pigeon River–Rainy Lake boundary between the United States and Canada.

Bayfield, promoted to captain (he eventually was made an admiral), spent the next two summers charting the coastline of Lake Superior and plumbing its depths. He took soundings of the bottom with a lead line consisting of a fourteen-pound ball of lead attached to a line with graduated markings on it. The lead ball was coated with sticky tallow so the leadsman, in addition to determining depth, could discover the nature of the bottom, whether rock, sand, or mud. This information, especially in the lake's bays, was important to mariners generally and to fishermen especially. An anchor would not hold on a smooth rock bottom, and its hooks could foul amidst large boulders. An anchor usually held well and released easily in sand or mud. Fishermen would also find a lake-bottom chart useful because trout and whitefish, like all fish, tend to favor specific habitats.

Bayfield returned to England after the 1825 season with his rough notes and drawings. Mapmakers in the British Admiralty's Hydrographic Office required two years to complete and publish the chart of Lake Superior. Bayfield would spend the rest of his naval career charting the St. Lawrence River and the Atlantic coast of Canada. In 1883 the retiring head of the Hydrographic Office paid him this tribute: "The Admiralty Surveying Service has produced good men, from Cook onwards, but I doubt whether the British Navy has ever possessed so gifted and zealous a Surveyor as Bayfield."

From Furs to Fish

After Congress in 1816 excluded British/Canadians from trapping furs on American territory, John Jacob Astor's American Fur Company had a virtual monopoly of the pelts taken from the rivers that flowed into the south and west shores of Lake Superior. Unfortunately, by that date the most valuable fur-bearing animals, beaver and otter, were pretty much trapped out. The company purchased muskrat pelts from Michigan and Wisconsin trappers, but that fur was regarded as much inferior to beaver for the making of hats, the item that had sustained the fur trade for more than a century. To make matters worse, European fashion was switching to silk for the top hats that gentlemen wore.

In 1823 Robert Stuart, an agent of the American Fur Company on Lake Superior, wrote to officer Ramsay Crooks to suggest that the company supplement its furs with fish. Stuart knew there was no market for Lake Superior fish on the American seaboard or in Europe; he proposed instead to exchange whitefish and trout in the port cities of Ohio (Toledo and Cleveland) for the corn, cheese, bacon, and peas that the company needed to supply its trappers in the woodlands west of Lake Superior. Although Crooks failed to respond positively to the idea, Stuart's proposal was the first look at the potential for commercial exploitation of the Lake Superior fishing grounds.

Crooks may have felt that a mundane trade in salted fish would not have appealed to the imperial-minded Astor. He stored the idea for future use, however. In 1834 Astor sold his interest in the American Fur Company, which was reorganized with Crooks as president. Shortly thereafter Crooks wrote to a friend in Washington asking him to inquire of the secretary of the treasury whether fish taken on the Canadian side of the great lakes but cured with American salt and transported in American vessels would be subject to a customs duty. "We have great hopes," Crooks noted, "of adding to the usual returns of our trade, a new and important item, in the Fisheries of Lake Superior." Unfortunately, there is no record of any response to Crooks's query.

Upon becoming president of American Fur, Crooks had shifted the company's western headquarters from Mackinac Island to La Pointe in Chequamegon Bay. This move brought the summer fur exchange closer to the Minnesota woodlands, where the best pelts were to be found, and gave the company a strategic port near Isle Royale and Wisconsin's rice-bearing sloughs, the best Lake Superior fishing grounds.

Crooks's plan was to build a schooner on Lake Superior to handle the company's traffic in furs and provisions. After the Hudson's Bay Company's schooner *Recovery* set off for service on Lake Huron in 1829 (a departure that involved a daring run down the Sault rapids), no full-rigged sailing vessels plied Lake Superior. The American Fur Company relied instead on Mackinaw boats. These vessels were eighteen to thirty

feet long, six to eight feet across at the beam, and pointed both fore and
aft. They had one or two masts carrying small lateen sails. Propelled by
both wind and oars, they were small enough to be run up on a beach
in bad weather. Crooks's schooner would displace about sixty-five of
the company's Mackinaw boatmen; to prevent the rival Hudson's Bay
Company from employing them, Crooks proposed to put them to work
catching fish.

The schooner *John Jacob Astor* was launched at Sault Ste. Marie on
August 3, 1835. That summer the new headquarters on Madeline Island
was completed, consisting of storehouses for furs and fish, a cluster of
dwellings for clerks and traders, and a pier for the sailing vessel. By the
end of the autumn fishing season, clerk Lyman Warren, in charge of the
station, reported 320 barrels of fish in his warehouse.

The fish were caught in nets close to shore. Lake trout came into
their shallow spawning grounds in mid-August, and whitefish arrived
a month later. From then until the lake froze over in late November,
company men kept busy setting nets, cleaning and packing the fish in
salt, and carrying the barrels to the warehouse. During the winter the
men cut trees, which coopers fashioned into barrel staves for the following summer's catch. The salt was brought by schooner from mines
in western New York.

In 1836 Crooks established a second fishing settlement at Grand
Portage. In charge of this post was Pierre Cote, who contracted with the
company to provide fish through 1840 on a five percent commission.
Cote employed two coopers and up to nine fishermen. The fishermen
set their nets along the sheltered west coast between Grand Marais and
the Pigeon River. In calm weather, they ventured the twenty-mile run to
Isle Royale. With a surplus of labor at La Pointe, Crooks in 1837 established yet another fishing settlement, this time on Isle Royale. Charles
Chaboillez, like Cote a métis or mixed-blood, was in charge of this station at a stipend of $350 a year. He employed fishermen at wages vary-
ing from $150 to $300 (depending, apparently, upon experience), and
he paid nine "freemen," who fished on their own, four dollars per two
hundred pounds of fish.

Expansion of the company's fishing operation resulted in dramatic
increases in output. American Fur shipped a thousand barrels of fish to

Though not the primary economic activity, fishing has long contributed to the diets of settlers along Lake Superior's shores. In this camp at Michipicoten, Ontario, 1850, by Elliot Cabot, nets dry on poles near log structures.

Detroit and other lake ports in 1836, double that number in 1837, four thousand barrels in 1838, and five thousand in 1839. In 1837 siscowet (a bait fish today) fetched fourteen dollars a barrel, whitefish and trout twelve dollars, and pickerel (northern pike) eight dollars.

The financial panic that struck eastern cities in May 1837 unfortunately ushered in a prolonged depression that eventually destroyed this first attempt at commercial fishing on the lake. By 1839 fish could be sold in the Ohio lake ports only on long-term credit. In desperation Crooks sent several hundred barrels by canal and riverboat into southern Ohio and Indiana but found that he could not compete—in either price or taste—with locally produced pork and beef. In 1840–41 attempts to sell fish (presumably for slaves) in the river ports from Memphis to New Orleans likewise failed.

The American Fur Company ceased its fishing operation in 1841 and declared bankruptcy the following year. It was almost thirty years before commercial fishing boats again appeared on Lake Superior.

The Copper Rush

In 1840, three years after Michigan achieved statehood, newly appointed state geologist Douglass Houghton, who had listened to Henry School-craft's tales of the Ontonagon copper rock and had accompanied Schoolcraft on a visit to the Keweenaw Peninsula, began a careful survey of the region that had generated tales of copper nodules since the days of Radisson and Groseilliers.

Copper was a versatile metal with a variety of uses, but it had no-where near the intrinsic value of gold. Its principal employment was industrial. It sheathed the bottoms of wooden sailing vessels, both to increase speed and to protect them from saltwater worms, and graced the roofs of many public buildings. Alloyed with zinc to make brass or with tin to make bronze, it went into candlesticks, cannons, and cook-ware. A national demand for copper existed, but the demand did not translate into high prices. A few might turn a profit from mining the metal, but many more would be financially ruined.

In 1841 Houghton reported on the district's mineral potential to the state legislature. The report's general tone was of scholarly restraint, and Houghton echoed the feeling among geologists that the presence of cop-per on the surface did not ensure the existence of minable ore beneath. But excitement oozed from his prose as he described what happened when he drilled a hole in a vein and filled it with gunpowder:

> In opening a vein with a single blast, I threw out nearly two tons of ore, and with this were many masses of native copper, from the most minute specks to about forty pounds in weight, which was the largest mass I obtained from that vein. Ores of silver occasionally occur with the copper, and in opening one vein small specks of native silver were observed.

Not surprisingly, his report caught the attention of Congress, which appropriated funds to purchase mineral lands from the Indians. The fol-lowing year the federal government negotiated a treaty with the Ojibwe by which they ceded the western half of Michigan's Upper Peninsula. The federal government, with Houghton's help, began a linear survey, by townships and sections, of the Keweenaw Peninsula. By the time the federal government opened a land office in Copper Harbor in 1843, the locations and boundaries of mine leases could be determined with some precision. By 1844 American Fur Company schooners were carrying boatloads of explorers, miners, and speculators to the Keweenaw, and the rush—a prelude to the gold rush of '49—was on!

An added stimulus to the copper fever occurred when the legendary copper rock was removed from its resting place on the banks of the Ontonagon River, a story of elemental drama that was reported with great gusto in the eastern press. Centerpiece of the story was Julius Eldred, a hardware merchant from Detroit, who decided he could improve his fortune by transporting the boulder east and exhibiting it. He visited the site in 1841 and purchased the rock for $150 from the Indians who lived along the river. By the time he was ready to move the boulder two years later, the Ojibwe had ceded the land to the federal government, and the army claimed ownership of the rock. Undaunted, Eldred purchased the rock a second time, paying an army colonel fourteen hundred dollars for it. He employed a crew of twenty ex-voyageurs and Indians, who cleared a path around the river's rapids and loaded the rock on a wagon equipped with railroad wheels. By picking up pieces of track after the wagon passed over and relaying them in front, they managed to transport the rock around the major rapids. They then built a raft for the remainder of the twenty-mile journey to Lake Superior.

Eldred chartered a sailing vessel to carry his treasure to Detroit, but when he stopped in Copper Harbor for supplies, he learned that the secretary of war had ordered the army to seize the rock as a national treasure. President John Tyler's secretary of the treasury wanted the boulder exhibited in the national museum being built with funds bequeathed to the government by James Smithson. Copper Harbor's commanding general generously allowed Eldred to accompany the boulder as far as Detroit, where he exhibited it briefly at twenty-five cents a ticket. After another sharp exchange that the press gleefully reported, the government gained control of the rock and shipped it east by way of the Erie Canal. In 1847 a conscience-tweaked Congress awarded Eldred the sum of $5,664.98 as reimbursement. Having been hacked and chipped for hundreds of years by Indians, explorers, and voyageurs, the boulder that eventually went on display at the Smithsonian weighed 3,700 pounds, its market value in copper a mere six hundred dollars. Its worth in publicity for the Keweenaw/Ontonagon mining district, on the other hand, was incalculable.

The copper-bearing rocks lying on the land's surface were quickly skimmed off, and eastern capitalists—mostly from Boston and New York—formed stock companies to sink mine shafts into the underground lodes. After filing a claim with the federal land office in Copper Harbor, the stock companies hired ex-voyageurs to squat on the claims while they assembled miners and drilling equipment. The squatters remained through the summer and autumn exploring season and were removed at winter's onset. Occasionally the rescue boat failed to appear, and the squatters faced a winter of hardship. French Canadian Charlie Mott and his Ojibwe wife, Angelique, were paid to squat on an Isle Royale mining claim in the summer of 1845. They were given only a short supply of flour, butter, and beans and a promise that they would be regularly provisioned and removed from the island before winter. Neither supply boat nor rescue boat ever appeared, and Charlie and Angelique were reduced to eating bark, roots, and insects. Charlie died of starvation; Angelique survived the winter by capturing rabbits in snares braided with her own hair. She later recalled how she was "tempted, O, how terribly I was tempted, to take Charlie and make soup of him."

The vessel that rescued Angelique was the *Algonquin,* built at Black River, Ohio, and purchased by the Boston Mining Company, which had several claims on Isle Royale. The fifty-ton schooner had been portaged around the falls at Sault Ste. Marie during the winter of 1839. Achille Cadotte (grandson of the fur trader) had shored up the *Algonquin* with timbers and used horses and a set of rollers to drag the vessel down what is today Water Street. Held up by periodic snowstorms, the mile-long portage took three and a half months, but it was the first of a parade of ships that "sailed on land" across the portage at the onset of the copper rush. In 1845 six schooners—one displacing 280 tons—and the steamer *Independence* made the portage around the falls, and the following year the first steamships—one a paddle wheeler, the other propeller driven—made the crossing to Lake Superior.

The first mine shafts were drilled in 1846, both near Copper Harbor at the tip of the peninsula. The Cliff Mine tapped into one of the region's

The Cliff Mine was one of the most productive on the Keweenaw, seen here in an 1850 sketch of the surface structures, including whims, a sorting house, and a kiln house.

richest veins of copper. By 1865 its owner, the Lake Superior Company, had paid stockholders dividends of $2.1 million on an initial investment of $110,000. Such payouts were a rarity, however, for very few of the copper veins on either Isle Royale or the Keweenaw resulted in any return on corporate investment.

The copper lodes—and hence the mine locations—ran along the spine of the Keweenaw Peninsula, some five or ten miles from the lakeshore and six hundred feet above it. Woodland trails connected the mines with the villages that sprang up below them—Copper Harbor, Eagle Harbor, Eagle River, Ontonagon. Hosting the government's land office, Copper Harbor was a tent city by 1843 and the site of an army post, Fort Wilkins, the following year. Congress had appropriated money for a fort on the Keweenaw to maintain peace with the Ojibwe and to preserve law and order among the fortune seekers. By 1845 Copper Harbor boasted the first "hotel" west of the Sault. In this log establishment, customers slept on bags of oats for twenty-five cents a night and were expected to provide their own blankets. For a few pennies more they could purchase a dinner of baked trout, pork and beans, and bread.

As the industry became more sophisticated, miners such as these men at the Hecla Mine were lifted up and down the mile-deep shafts in cars on tracks.

Rare in metallurgy, the copper found in the Keweenaw/Isle Royale region was in pure form, not an ore. Most metals—iron ore, for instance—occur in nature as compounds with oxygen or sulfur. Michigan copper was unalloyed, but—except for the fist-sized nodules that were easily mined and sent directly to a smelter—most of the copper consisted of tiny flakes imbedded in rock. Even one of the richest mines, that of the Quincy Mining Company near Portage Lake, yielded rock that was about two percent copper and 98 percent waste. The rock had to be taken to a stamping mill—the first was built at Eagle River in 1845—to be crushed. The copper, which had a specific gravity greater than the rock, was separated by washing and jiggling, in much the same way that western prospectors panned for gold. The copper was then sent to a smelter to be melted into pure ingots. The nearest smelter—until Hancock on Portage Lake acquired one in 1860—was in Detroit.

The movement of men and equipment to the mines, and copper out, gave rise to a subsidiary industry: road building. Prior to the copper rush, the Keweenaw Peninsula was almost impassable, even to foot traffic. The peninsula was a morass of muddy bogs and rock cliffs, the whole covered with a dense forest of cedars, pines, and hardwoods. The famous Portage Trail across the peninsula was a nearly all-water route, via the Portage River and Portage Lake. The miners first built trails connecting the mines with lakeshore villages. They then connected the mines with one another, and by 1855 a patched-together road extended down the spine of the peninsula from Copper Harbor to Ontonagon, though it was so stump filled as to be passable only to a person on horseback or on foot.

Steam engines to power the drills and lift copper out of the mine shafts were the next improvement. The first was installed on a mine near Eagle River in 1845; a decade later, there were forty-eight in the district. In 1867 the Hecla Mine (later to become part of Calumet and Hecla, the largest of all Michigan mining companies) built the peninsula's first steam railroad, a four-mile stretch of track from its mine to its stamping mill on Torch Lake (an arm of Portage Lake). By 1890 the peninsula had a network of railroads connecting mines, stamping mills, and smelting furnaces, and the mining companies were shipping their product not only by lake steamer but by rail to Milwaukee and Chicago.

Copper was melted into ingots for transportation by rail or ship.

The two most profitable copper veins were the Cliff Mine at the tip of the peninsula and the Minesota Mine (named at a time when the present state of Minnesota lay buried and undefined inside the Wisconsin Territory) in the Ontonagon valley. Both of these bonanzas were exhausted by 1870. In the 1850s the Quincy Mine, near Portage Lake in the center of the peninsula, exploited a different kind of rock formation that contained, instead of veins of copper, billions of flecks of the mineral more or less evenly distributed throughout the conglomerate rock. The Quincy's success gave rise to the twin cities of Hancock and Houghton on each side of Portage Lake. By 1860 the Portage River channel had been dredged to allow lake steamers to dock at the two mill towns. Within another decade a twenty-two-mile ship canal had been dug, with financing from Congress and the state of Michigan, across the peninsula. In 1871, a year after the Cliff and Minesota operations shut down, the Calumet and Hecla Mining Company was born. Exploiting the conglomerate in the vicinity of Portage Lake, Calumet and Hecla would become one of the world's richest and most successful mining companies.

In 1886 the state chartered the Michigan College of Mines (now Michigan Technological University) at Houghton to train young men for managerial positions in the copper mines. With ever larger and more sophisticated machinery, the mines went ever deeper in their pursuit of the red metal. Some of the Calumet and Hecla mines extended more than a mile into the earth by the turn of the century. The Michigan mines reached a peak output around 1910 and thereafter went into a slow decline as they exhausted the copper supply. Mines closed one after another in the 1920s and '30s, and the last of the great operations, that of Calumet and Hecla, shut down in 1969.

In the meantime, the copper rush of the 1840s and '50s had an enormous impact on the shipping of the blue water highway, as steam-driven steel carriers replaced the wooden-walled ships that dated from the fur trade. The first step in this transportation revolution was to eliminate the portage bottleneck at Sault Ste. Marie.

The Sault Canal

The Canada-based North West Company had built a canal around the falls in 1797, but it was a crude ditch two feet deep, capable of carrying only canoes and bateaux. It nevertheless served the fur company well until a band of American militia destroyed it during the War of 1812. No one gave further thought to a canal at the Sault until Michigan became a state in 1837. In that year the legislature sent an engineer to the falls; he reported that the rock in the vicinity was easily removed sandstone. What he apparently did not realize was that the layer of sandstone rested on the granitic bedrock of the Canadian Shield, a circumstance that would ultimately double the cost of building a canal.

In 1839 the Michigan legislature petitioned Congress for a grant of public land to help finance construction of a canal. (Congress had used land, the nation's most abundant resource, as a subsidy for national development ever since it set aside parcels for public schools in the Northwest Ordinance of 1785.) A bill to grant Michigan one hundred thousand acres of federal land (that is, land purchased from the Indians but not yet opened to public sale) reached the floor of the U.S. Senate in spring 1840. There, curiously enough, the bill ran into the steadfast opposition of Henry Clay, who called the project "a work beyond the remotest settlement of the United States, if not the moon."

"Internal improvements" (federal subsidies for construction of roads and canals) had been a feature of Clay's political platform for more than a decade, but in 1840 he had his eye on the Whig presidential nomination to run against Democrat Martin Van Buren. Since Van Buren, a disciple of Andrew Jackson, was opposed to any sort of government interaction with private enterprise, Clay may have been trimming his political platform to broaden his voter appeal. Both Clay and Michigan lost. The Whig Party nominated instead William Henry Harrison, "Old Tippecanoe," to oppose Van Buren, and the Michigan land grant died in the Senate.

A succession of southern presidents—John Tyler, James K. Polk, Zachary Taylor—prevented any further discussion of a Sault canal, or any other internal improvements, for the next decade. Southerners opposed the employment of federal power and money as a matter of principle, for, as one congressman remarked, "If the government can build roads and canals, it can free slaves."

The untimely death of President Taylor in 1850 brought Millard Fillmore to the White House. A New Yorker whose home, Buffalo, was the terminus for the Erie Canal, Fillmore was a friend to federally financed internal improvements. By that date, moreover, state financing of roads and canals was no longer possible. In the heyday of canal building (following the success of the Erie), Ohio, Indiana, and Illinois had nearly bankrupted themselves financing the construction of canals connecting the Great Lakes with the Ohio and Mississippi rivers. Profiting by that folly, Wisconsin in 1848 and Michigan in 1850 drafted constitutions that prohibited the state from participating in or loaning money to an internal improvement project.

In 1852, with Fillmore's term coming to an end and the likelihood that the Democrats would win the coming presidential election, Michigan again asked Congress for a federal land grant. Eastern businessmen with investments in copper and the Michigan Central Railroad added their support. Congress approved a bill granting Michigan 750,000 acres of public land, and President Fillmore signed it into law. The grant, however, was contingent upon completion of the canal, and since Michigan could not borrow money for such a purpose, a privately owned construction company would have to be formed and private investors found. The inducement to investment was that a canal company would have the right to choose which public lands it wanted and to resell them

 **VISITING HISTORY**

Coppertown, USA, Mining Museum (Red Jacket Road, off Highway 41, Calumet, Michigan) offers a collection of artifacts and photographs of mining history in a building that was once part of the Calumet and Hecla Mine.

The **Quincy Mine** complex (Highway 41, north up the hill from Hancock, Michigan) contains the restored shaft–rock house and mile-deep elevator of the most productive of Michigan's copper mines.

The **Tower of History** (Portage Avenue and Johnson Street, Sault Ste. Marie, Michigan) is a two-hundred-foot-high observation deck that provides a panoramic view of the city and the canal.

Government Park (Portage Avenue, Sault Ste. Marie, Michigan) at the American Locks is operated by the U.S. Army Corps of Engineers. Although there is no public access to the locks themselves, the park has an observation deck for viewing passing ships.

St. Marys River Boardwalk (Sault Ste. Marie, Ontario) stretches along the city's rejuvenated waterfront from the civic center (which has a magnificent penthouse observation gallery) to the Canadian Lock.

Museum Ship S.S. *Valley Camp* (Sault Ste. Marie, Michigan) is a retired Great Lakes freighter and maritime museum located at the southern end of the city's mile-long Waterfront Pathway.

at its leisure. Even at the government minimum price of $1.25 an acre, the 750,000-acre grant was worth one million dollars, more than double the estimated $450,000 cost to build a canal. (As it turned out, canal construction costs came to almost a million, due in part to the granite bedrock that had to be moved.)

While eastern businessmen worked at forming a canal company, Augustus Canfield, a captain in the Army Corps of Topographical Engineers and son-in-law to Lewis Cass, former governor and current U.S. senator from Michigan, sailed to the Sault to survey the landscape and draft a general plan for a canal. Canfield's survey was flawed—he failed to detect the bedrock under the sandstone—but his plan was blessed with foresight. Congress had provided that the canal's two locks (spanning the twenty-two-foot drop in the rapids) measure at least 60 feet wide and 250 feet long. Anticipating an increase in vessel size, as iron steamships came increasingly into use on the lake, Canfield proposed locks 70 feet wide and 300 feet long. That proposal—extended by the Michigan legislature to 350 feet—was the most vital decision in the story of the canal, for it governed ship construction on the Great Lakes for the next thirty years, until the locks were rebuilt by the U.S. government in 1881.

In the spring of 1853 the state of New York granted a charter to the St. Marys Falls Ship Canal Company with power to enter into a contract with the state of Michigan to construct a canal and, upon its completion, to improve or sell the public lands granted by Congress. President of the company was Erastus Corning, an Albany businessman with experience in building railroads, including the Michigan Central, which was planned to connect Detroit with the Straits of Mackinac. The capital stock of the corporation was four hundred thousand dollars; most of the investors were New Yorkers. On May 19, 1853, the company entered into a contract with the state of Michigan, agreeing to complete a canal in precisely two years.

Construction began that summer. The workforce, which numbered about sixteen hundred at any one time, consisted mostly of newly arrived Irish and German immigrants. Many were housed in company-built barracks, fifty men to a log house, with a strong and dominant male in each to supervise cooking and cleaning. Charles T. Harvey, the company's

An essential link: the locks at Sault Ste. Marie make possible navigation from Lake Superior to the St. Marys River and Lake Huron. This steamer made the passage in about 1890.

agent in charge of construction, was reluctant to employ females in the uncouth atmosphere. Unskilled workers who boarded with the company received twenty dollars a month. Masons, who installed the canal's limestone walls, made three dollars a day and generally boarded in town. All workers complained that, after a month of monotonous labor, there was nothing to spend their money on in that town of two hundred French and mixed-blood Indians—except whiskey.

Construction ceased in the winter, and many workers sought employment in the Lower Peninsula's lumber camps. Blasting through the granite bedrock slowed construction and added greatly to expenses. The canal company ran through its capital and had to assess its stockholders an additional five hundred thousand dollars to complete the job. The hardwood forests in the vicinity of the Sault yielded timber good only for firewood, and the company had to buy pine timbers for the locks from lumber companies in the Lower Peninsula. Corning's iron foundry in Albany supplied ironware for the locks as well as tools for the masons

PORT CITY

The canals of **Sault Ste. Marie, Ontario,** and **Sault Ste. Marie, Michigan,** have made these cities central shipping points since the nineteenth century, and today ship traffic remains an important component of the cities' economies. The Ontario canal caters to pleasure craft, while the U.S. canal provides passage to ships from all corners of the globe and reigns as the most-visited site on the lake. The Ontario side, with a population of nearly seventy-five thousand, dominates the Michigan city of 16,500 and offers industry, shopping, and culture.

───────────

and woodcutters. No one questioned Corning's personal enrichment; *conflict of interest* was not part of the day's vocabulary.

As the deadline approached in the spring of 1855, much remained to be done. The bedrock had not been smoothly blasted, and the gates of the locks could not hold water—either in or out. The masonry work on the canal walls was faulty in some places, incomplete in others. In January the canal company, desperate for money, informed the state that the canal was substantially completed and asked for its 750,000 acres. The legislature balked at that request, but it did establish a canal commission to oversee operations once the facility was in state hands. In February the federal land office in Washington sent the patents for 750,000 acres to the Michigan secretary of state in Lansing. In early May, ice finally cleared from the waters of the St. Marys River, allowing the first test of the canal's banks and locks.

The state commissioners trickled into the Sault, missing the May 19 deadline, and, with only the most casual inspection of the works, handed Corning a document on May 21 certifying that "said canal has been constructed within two years within the making of the contract . . . to our satisfaction and acceptance." State commissioners and canal officers then repaired to Lansing, where the state turned over the right to 750,000 acres of Michigan lands, slightly more than two percent of the state's entire land surface. The first vessel to use the canal on June 18,

1855, was a sailing schooner, pulled through the locks by Lady Elgin, the canal mule, with a shipload of miners and barrels of whiskey destined for the copper fields of the Keweenaw.

The total cost of constructing the canal was $913,492, and the only reimbursement to the company was the land grant. The state took over operation of the canal, charging four cents a ton for each ship's enrolled tonnage. Since tonnage was a matter of water displacement rather than size of cargo, this figure had to be revised when steel ships carrying iron ore replaced the wooden sailing ships with their cargoes of grain and whiskey. (While the capacity of a merchant vessel is normally measured in units of one hundred cubic feet of water, canal tolls were based on "register tons," where one ton equaled one hundred cubic feet of enclosed space within the vessel.)

The canal company stockholders nevertheless did well by themselves. They employed "landlookers" to discover the best timber and mineral lands in the state. Among their acquisitions were rich pinelands in the Lower Peninsula and seemingly barren rock in the vicinity of Portage Lake on the Keweenaw that eventually became the site of several Calumet and Hecla copper mines. It has been estimated that the immediate return to canal company stockholders was 50 percent on their investment. After the canal company was dissolved, many stockholders formed a new company to dispose of the remaining lands, and the returns on those sales over the next half century amounted to millions.

The state of Michigan operated the canal until 1881, when the increasing flow of iron ore and grain required bigger carriers and a canal of larger proportions. The Army Corps of Engineers took over in that year and eventually replaced the original lock with four locks that speeded passage and accommodated larger ships. In 1895 Canada built a canal on its side of the river, and locks in both canals were enlarged four times in the twentieth century, most recently in 1969. By the mid-twentieth century, the Sault canals were handling more shipping tonnage annually than the other three great canals of the world—Panama, Suez, and Kiel—combined.

CHAPTER FIVE

BLUE WATER HIGHWAY

IN SEPTEMBER 1844, while the Keweenaw copper rush was gaining momentum, a team of federal surveyors was drawing township and section lines along the mountainous spine of Michigan's Upper Peninsula. In the vicinity of Teal Lake, they noticed their compass needles moving crazily, pointing east sometimes, then ranging to the west or even due south. Realizing there must be iron nearby, William A. Burt told his men, "Boys, look around and see what you can find." The men chipped hunks of iron ore from rocky outcrops and hauled as much as they could carry back to their base at Sault Ste. Marie.

Burt's report to the government contained only a casual reference to the discovery of iron—perhaps because he did not realize the extent of the deposit—but Jacob Houghton, the barometer man in Burt's party and brother of the state geologist, was more excited. In 1846 he published a book, *The Mineral Region of Lake Superior,* in which he quoted brother Douglass (who had drowned in Lake Superior the previous year) that "the bed of iron" discovered by Burt's party "will compare favorably, both for extent and quality, with any known in our country."

Even before Houghton published his book, the stories told by members of Burt's party generated considerable excitement in Sault Ste. Marie. In summer 1845 the rumors attracted the attention of Philo M. Everett, a shopkeeper from Jackson, Michigan. Everett and a dozen of his neighbors had formed themselves into the Jackson Iron Mining Company to file copper claims on the Keweenaw. Everett and three other company members were passing through the Sault on their way to the copper country when they heard tales of "iron mountains" to the west. Deflected from their mission, they rowed along the lakeshore from the Sault to the mouth of the Carp River and headed up into the iron range. With the help of local Indians, who resided near a spot they called *Ishpeming* ("Upper"), Everett located the iron outcrops Burt's men had found. He returned to the Sault and filed a mining claim, paying the government $2.50 an acre for land that would yield, before operations ceased in 1924, five million tons of ore. He wrote breathlessly to his Jackson friends that their holdings contained "a mountain of solid iron ore, 150 feet high. The ore looks as bright as a bar of iron just broken." Everett was not exaggerating, for the ore was assayed to contain as much as 50 percent pure iron.

Because the Jackson Company's claim was seven miles from Lake Superior, Everett and his associates never considered the possibility of shipping out the raw ore. They planned instead to bring a forge to the mine and reduce the ore to bars of pig iron using charcoal from the local hardwood forest. Buying the equipment and hauling it around the falls of the Carp River took two years; the first iron bars were sent to the mouth of the Carp in February 1848. By that date, prospectors had found another outcrop, later named Cleveland Mountain, two miles to the west of the Jackson mine. This group, organized as the Marquette Iron Company, built a forge at the mouth of the Carp River, erected a pair of log houses amidst the wigwams of a handful of Ojibwe, and called their settlement Marquette.

Neither the Jackson forge nor the Marquette forge returned a profit. Because there were no roads, the ore could be carried to the lakeshore only in the winter on sleds. The horses pulling the sleds consumed hay imported from the Detroit area at forty dollars a ton. Maple and birch were scarce in the vicinity of Marquette, and woodsmen, usually Indians, ranged into the hills to cut hardwoods and burn them into charcoal in open pits. The Marquette forge went into operation in 1850, and the company discovered that it cost two hundred dollars a ton to produce bars of iron and ship them to Pittsburgh's steel mills. In Pittsburgh, the market price for iron was only eighty dollars a ton.

About the same time, a group of investors in Cleveland obtained a corporate charter from the Michigan legislature, and over the next three years the Cleveland Iron Company acquired the Marquette company's forges and mine locations. The Cleveland men abandoned the expensive process of forging the ore into iron and decided instead to ship the raw ore to furnaces in Ohio and Pennsylvania that were producing iron with anthracite coal. By 1855 they had completed a plank road from the mines to the booming village of Marquette, and within a year they shipped over eleven thousand tons of ore out of that port. Within another year, iron rails lay on top of the wooden planks and a twenty-five ton steam engine, made in New Jersey, was bringing down from the range twelve hundred tons a day.

The iron range attracted immigrants with mining skills: Germans from the Ruhr Valley, English from Cornwall and Wales. Ishpeming was founded in 1856, and Marquette incorporated as a village three years later, its population by then over two thousand. Marquette's first ore dock was made of logs, sand, and gravel, capable of handling only one small ship at a time. Sweating workmen pushed the ore onto the dock in wheelbarrows and dumped it into the vessel's hold. After a storm washed the dock into the bay, the Cleveland Company built the first modern ore dock. It consisted of a series of log cribs, each twenty feet square and filled with heavy stone. The cribs extended four hundred feet into the lake and supported a trestle with iron tracks for the ore cars. Under the trestle was a series of pockets with chutes that slanted out over the vessels being loaded. The ore could thus be dumped directly from the railroad cars into the ore boats. The dock, capable of loading four vessels at the same time, opened on June 22, 1859.

The opening of the Sault Ste. Marie canal drastically reduced the cost of shipping the ore. In 1855 the mining companies spent three dollars per ton to move the ore from the range to Marquette and five dollars to ship it from Marquette to the Lake Erie ports of Cleveland and Buffalo. By 1858 the steam railroad reduced the cost to Marquette to eighty-seven cents a ton and the Sault canal cut the lake transport to two dollars a ton. In that year an Ohio shipbuilder began designing schooners expressly for the purpose of carrying ore. Previously, ship captains had mingled the ore with barrels of fish and other goods being transported east.

Wooden sailing ships did not make satisfactory ore boats: the masts, booms, and lines interfered with the loading of bulk cargo. Even the

G. N. Ore Docks, Superior, Wis.

Modern ore docks, this one in Superior in 1910, simplified the process of filling ore boats and increased port cities' efficiency at moving the region's mineral wealth to eastern markets.

largest ones' capacity was only three to four hundred tons. In the late 1860s, Ohio shipyards began designing steamships for the ore trade. Prototypes of twentieth-century ore boats, they had a pilothouse in the bow, engines and crew quarters in the rear, and a line of hatches in the middle for the unobstructed handling of ore. Initially made of wood and equipped with auxiliary sails, the ore boats evolved into iron and steel by the early 1880s. In 1872 the Cleveland Company acquired its own fleet of steamers, each capable of carrying a thousand tons of ore.

The Gogebic Range

Marquette remained the only iron ore port on Lake Superior until 1876, when L'Anse, at the head of Keweenaw Bay, built an ore dock. L'Anse became the ore shipping port for new mines opened to the west of the Marquette Range on the Upper Peninsula's mountainous spine. Farther west still lay the Gogebic Range, which straddles the Michigan-Wisconsin border and joins Wisconsin's Northern Highlands, the watershed between Lake Superior and the Mississippi River. Although surveyors noted the presence of high-quality iron ore in the Gogebic as early as 1858, an "iron rush" failed to develop. In 1872 Nathaniel D. Moore, prospecting along the Montreal River, which forms the boundary between Michigan and Wisconsin, noticed hematite earth around the roots of a windfall tree. He formed the Iron Chief Mining Company and acquired a large section of range property on the Wisconsin side of the river. However, it was another decade before he amassed enough capital to open a mine. The success of Moore's operation triggered a mining boom in the mid-1880s that sprouted the raucous villages of Ironwood and Hurley, on either side of the Montreal River, and a new shipping port, Ashland, on Lake Superior.

The settlement that ultimately became Ashland, at the head of Chequamegon Bay, originated in the rumors of iron that stemmed from the 1848–52 survey of the Gogebic Range. Charles Whittlesey, the geologist who had explored the range and noted its proximity to the "natural harbor" of Chequamegon Bay, advised his brother Asaph, whose candle and soap business in Peoria, Illinois, had burned to the ground, to venture to the bay and start life anew. Asaph and his family arrived at La Pointe on Madeline Island in June 1854 and found it a "beautiful town" populated by a "curious mixture of Americans, Jews, Germans, French, and Austrians." The village apparently subsisted on a combination of fishing, fur trading, and tourism.

During the summer Whittlesey and two companions explored the bay's south shore and determined that the mouth of Fish Creek was a suitable site for a town. It would serve as a shipping port for any ore that might be found in the Gogebic Range, and it was a logical terminus for the Fox River–Lake Superior railroad then being planned. In October 1854 the partners purchased 280 acres from the government and platted the site as the Town of Ashland. The reason for choosing that name remains a mystery, but it seems likely that Whittlesey or one of his partners was a fan of Senator Henry Clay, whose home was Ashland, Kentucky. Before the snows set in, there were three cabins on the shore near Fish Creek. Whittlesey, whose vision was nothing if not grandiose, described his abode as one "of massive proportions . . . the most aristocratic house in the place."

During the winter the Whittlesey "mansion" hosted the community's first religious service, conducted by a preacher from the Odanah Indian mission, and in the spring of 1855 it became the village post office, with

Asaph as postmaster. By 1856 the town had acquired a saloon and a general store. Settlers trickled in, attracted by the boomtown mentality and the perceived healthfulness of the bay. In 1858 the bustling community had its first murder, as a resident was shot to death in a tavern brawl. The state legislature formed Ashland County with the village as county seat in 1860. At that point it had a population of 67: 41 adults and 26 children.

That was the beginning and the end of "old Ashland." By 1863 the site was a ghost town, and the county seat had been transferred to La Pointe. No nearby iron ore had been found, and the Civil War interrupted plans for a railroad. The first settlers, most of them interested only in speculating in urban lots, moved elsewhere in search of fortune. Through the decade of the 1860s, the only human presence in Ashland was a farm family from the Marengo River valley who treated one of the abandoned dwellings as a summer "fish house."

After the war, survey parties laid out a route for what would become the Wisconsin Central Railroad, from Manitowoc to Stevens Point to Park Falls. In 1871 the railroad selected Chequamegon Bay as its terminus on Lake Superior, and a survey was run from Ashland south to a gap in the Highlands (present-day Mellen). The prospect of a railroad link to Milwaukee and Chicago resurrected the boom mentality, and a "new Ashland" was born as old settlers, including Asaph Whittlesey, returned to their abandoned cabins and new arrivals pitched tents. By the end of 1872 the community had a population of three hundred and boasted a post office, a library, a brewery, and a newspaper. Its principal industry was a sawmill that produced lumber for the mushrooming copper cities on the Keweenaw and for a growing fishery on Isle Royale. Iron ore still lay hidden in the Gogebic hills.

The panic of 1873 delayed railroad construction, but a line connecting Ashland with the Fox River valley and ports on Lake Michigan was finally completed in June 1877. Fittingly, Asaph Whittlesey drove the last spike and made a short speech. Characteristic of the booster mentality that pervaded nineteenth-century America, executives of the Wisconsin Central did not raise the question of what freight the railroad might carry until after they completed the line. White and red pine, the favored woods for housing construction, grew in profusion in the river valleys south of the Marquette-Gogebic-Highland mountain chain, but those trees were scarce in the "spruce-moose biome" of Lake Superior. Accordingly, Ashland's sawmills could barely keep up with the demand for lumber in cities along the lake and had little surplus to send to Milwaukee or Chicago. Iron ore, if and when discovered, was more economically shipped by lake freighter than by rail. What to do for revenue?

 **VISITING HISTORY**

The **Marquette Historic District** (Arch and Ridge Streets, Marquette, Michigan) comprises the opulent mansions of the city's nineteenth-century business elite.

The **Marquette County History Museum** (North Front Street, Marquette, Michigan) exhibits on subjects ranging from Indian culture to the iron ore boom.

The **Downtown Ashland Tour** (Ashland, Wisconsin) begins with the Hotel Chequamegon, a reconstruction of the original hotel built in 1877 by the Wisconsin Central Railroad, and features nineteenth-century buildings of locally quarried brown sandstone, including the mansions of the city's commercial elite, the Soo Line Depot, and the original Ashland post office.

The **Ashland Ore Dock** (Ashland, Wisconsin), built in 1916, is 1,800 feet long and eighty feet high. At one time the city was home to five such docks.

The **Iron County Courthouse/Museum** (Iron Street, Hurley, Wisconsin), built in 1892–93 of red sandstone in the Romanesque Style, contains memorabilia of Hurley's turbulent mining and logging past.

The **Chicago and Northwestern Depot** (Suffolk and Lowell Streets, Ironwood, Michigan) is being developed into a museum of Ironwood's mining and lumbering history by the Ironwood Historical Society.

The Chequamegon Hotel, built by the Wisconsin Central Railroad and opened in 1877, drew visitors to the booming town of Ashland.

Noting that La Pointe did a nice tourist business, railroad executives announced in spring 1877 that they planned a large resort hotel in Ashland. The Chequamegon Hotel, three stories high, surrounded with a wide veranda, opened on the first of August, while the ecstatic *Ashland Press* predicted that the city would become "the Saratoga of the Northwest." A visitor from Green Bay in September noted that the hotel "is overflowing and spilling over pretty much all the time with an excess of pleasure seekers." The *Ashland Press* boosted the new industry with headlines like "Ashland and Vicinity: The Summer Resort of the West." Railroad executives hastened to enlarge the hotel, and by 1881 it featured one hundred rooms with gas lighting and "all modern improvements such as electric bells, bath rooms, closets, steam laundry, etc."

In 1884 soft red hematite ore was rediscovered in the lands along the Montreal River, including the property claimed in 1872 by Nathaniel D. Moore. The next three years witnessed the greatest mining boom in Wisconsin's history. At its height, twenty-two mining companies had been formed, their stockholders principally in Milwaukee and cities of the Fox River valley. Speculation drove the nominal value of companies' capital stock to forty million dollars. A multimillionaire overnight, Nat Moore arrayed himself in a gaudy vest adorned with black onyx buttons set with diamonds. The crash came in late 1887, when investors realized that returns from ore shipments did not justify the stocks' high price. In the ensuing panic, Moore went under, black onyx buttons and all.

Amid the turmoil, however, ore production increased steadily. The first shipments went southeast to Escanaba on Lake Michigan, via a line that had been built to serve the Marquette and Menominee ranges. In 1885 the Milwaukee, South Shore and Western Railroad completed a much shorter line from the Montreal River to Ashland, where the company built a huge ore dock. The first ore shipment of thirteen hundred tons went out on a barge pulled by a steam-bulk freighter. By 1890 Ashland was shipping three million tons of ore a season.

The twin "iron cities" of Ironwood and Hurley were carved out of the woods with an influx of miners and lumberjacks. Ironwood, on the

 **PORT CITIES**

Marquette—the largest city in Michigan's Upper Peninsula—earned its place as a prominent Lake Superior port thanks to the mineral wealth of the Marquette Range. The city of approximately twenty thousand continues to export ore and import coal, but its nineteenth-century heyday is long past. It remains central to the region, however, home to Northern Michigan University and a hub for services, shopping, medicine, and tourism.

After its rebirth, **Ashland** made the most of its railroad connections and port location, exporting lumber and "Ashland Stone" from its brownstone quarries and eventually claiming a spot as the lake's largest shipper of ore. Today's town of nearly nine thousand, home to Northland College, focuses less on shipping and more on manufacturing, logging, medical services, and tourism.

Ironwood was home to miners and lumberjacks. This view is Aurora Street looking west in May 1886.

Michigan side of the Montreal River, was the more respectable of the two. It was named not for the tree whose wood is so hard that it was used for wagon axle parts but for a mine captain nicknamed "Iron" Wood. Hurley, on the Wisconsin side, featured fireproof brick taverns along duckboard sidewalks covered with red hematite dust. Its infamous Silver Street was lined with saloons, dance halls, gambling dens, and brothels. Ironwood could afford to be staid because Hurley, whose population by the end of the decade blossomed to seven thousand, afforded sin enough for the entire north country.

Although the Gogebic Range was mined until the 1940s, Ashland reached a population peak of 14,500 in 1905. Its gradual decline thereafter reflected the superior quality of ore found yet farther west, in Minnesota's Mesabi Range.

Superior, Duluth, Two Harbors, and the Mesabi

In 1854 the federal government purchased from the Ojibwe the lands along Lake Superior's south shore, including the sites that would become Ashland, Superior, and Duluth, for about a million dollars in annuities.

The two cities at the end of the lake therefore made their appearance about the same time as Ashland.

Superior, Wisconsin, was to be another Chicago. The spectacular growth of Chicago in the 1840s caught the attention of investors across the country. The city's progress was clearly due to its choice location: a port at the foot of Lake Michigan and the railroad hub of the Middle West. Superior seemed to offer the same advantages: a natural harbor at the western tip of Lake Superior and a potential hub for a railroad network extending into the western plains. After Congress in 1852 made a land grant to the state of Michigan for a shipping canal around the Falls of St. Marys, Senators Stephen A. Douglas of Illinois and Robert J. Walker of Mississippi, both heavily invested in western railroads, recognized the potential of a port at the western end of Lake Superior. In league with several other members of Congress, they filed claims for a town site on Superior Bay. A consortium of lawyers from St. Paul and a trio of copper prospectors from Ontonagon also filed claims in the area, and in 1854 the three groups joined together as the "Proprietors of Superior City." Of the eighteen proprietors, seven were members of Congress.

The combined claims totaled 5,327 acres, and city lots and streets were platted over the next three years. The newborn city, which had a population of 385 by the summer of 1855, contained twenty-four avenues and thirty-three streets. Town lots were twenty-five by one hundred feet, with many set aside for schools, churches, and parks. Most of the early arrivals were themselves speculators, and lot prices escalated to as much as $1,500 each. Senator Douglas, whose initial investment was no more that $2,500, reportedly sold his proprietary share for $135,000.

Although the "city" was little more than a pipe dream in 1855, as the seat of newly created Douglas County it boasted a post office, a federal land office, and a newspaper. As in Ashland, the chief function of the paper, the *Superior Chronicle,* was to promote the town. In the first issue the editors declared that "the site of the town of Superior is one of the most beautiful in the country" and predicted that, because it was at the head of lake navigation, "Superior is destined to be the most important point on the Lake." The proprietors' advertisement in the same issue was even more grand, declaring that Superior's location and harbor "is equalled in prospective importance by Chicago only."

Superior, like many other western towns, experienced extensive growth after the railroads arrived. A cart of sewer tiles (ca. 1890) makes its way along a street lined with attractions and shops, including an opera house and a shoemaker.

Regular steamboat service linking Superior with Chicago and other lake ports began in the summer of 1855, but the dreams of Superior's boosters could be realized only with the construction of railroads linking it to the farm- and timberlands of the St. Croix and Mississippi river valleys. A St. Croix and Superior Railroad Company was formed in 1856 and obtained a land grant to finance construction. The railroad surveyed a line from Hudson, Wisconsin (which was connected by rail to St. Paul), to Superior, but construction was forestalled by the panic of 1857 and the ensuing depression. The city's population, which according to the *Chronicle* had reached three thousand in 1857, fell to 531 in 1860, with 56 percent of the buildings unoccupied.

When Minnesota finally completed a railroad line between St. Paul and Lake Superior in 1870, its terminal was Duluth, rather than Superior. The city of Superior did not obtain rail service until 1881, when the Northern Pacific passed through, building a line from Duluth to Ashland.

Superior's growth thereafter was a spillover from the immense traffic in western grain and timber passing through Duluth.

Duluth, on the Minnesota side of the St. Louis River, would ultimately stretch from the river's marshes up the steep gabbro-rock hills that mark Minnesota's North Shore. The "scenic location" much discussed by Superior's boosters referred not to the city's own relatively flat and low-lying site but to its view across the bay to the hills that would become Duluth.

The American Fur Company's post at Fond du Lac, at the head of navigation on the St. Louis River, became an Indian mission (initially Catholic, later Presbyterian) in the 1830s. The last missionary departed in 1849, and the site was deserted, save for a few Indian teepees, because the river's estuary into Lake Superior was too shallow for lake-draft steamboats. Modern Duluth began in 1852 when George Stuntz (later a major figure in the development of Minnesota's iron ranges) built a

VISITING HISTORY

The **Burlington Northern Ore Docks** (off Highway 2/53, Superior, Wisconsin), dating from 1892, are still in operation, loading taconite pellets from Minnesota's Mesabi Range.

The **Whaleback Ore Carrier** *Meteor* (Barker's Island, off Highway 2/53, Superior, Wisconsin) is the last remaining cigar-shaped ore carrier built in the 1890s and houses an excellent maritime museum.

The elegant **Fairlawn Mansion Museum** (Second Street, Superior, Wisconsin), the home of a nineteenth-century lumber baron, is maintained by the Douglas County Historical Society.

The **Osaugie Trail** (Superior, Wisconsin) is a paved five-mile pathway along the city's waterfront. Motorized visitors can connect to the **Tri-County Corridor,** an unpaved multi-use trail through Douglas, Bayfield, and Ashland counties.

Looking over Minnesota Point, ca. 1885, shows a lighthouse at the canal entrance and ships arriving and departing the Duluth-Superior harbor.

trading post on Minnesota Point, a long narrow sandbar (much like Long Island in Chequamegon Bay) that extended from the Minnesota shore to an inlet opposite the village of Superior. In 1855, a year after the federal government cleared the site's Indian title, Stuntz's community became the town of Duluth and obtained a federal post office.

Duluth did not share the boom-and-bust cycle of Superior and Ashland, in part because it was founded in the year of financial panic. By the federal census of 1860, the village had only eighty residents. Like Superior and Ashland, it became a ghost town during the Civil War. In 1865 a newcomer, whom the government paid two hundred dollars a year to carry mail to the pioneer families along the St. Louis River, wrote: "All the houses then in Duluth were unoccupied, and had been for three years, so I had a perfect freedom for selection." There were then only two other families in the community, and, because there were no stores, they had to travel to Superior for supplies.

In 1870 the Lake Superior and Mississippi Railroad completed construction of a line linking Duluth to St. Paul, and the city began to prosper. Within a year it boasted six hotels "ready for summer guests." In 1871 the city, with help from the railroads, dredged a 250-foot canal across the base of Minnesota Point, allowing freighters to dock at Duluth without the long detour through Superior Bay. Loggers moved into the pinelands of the upper Mississippi during the 1870s, and Duluth became a

VISITING HISTORY

Skyline Parkway (begins off Interstate 35 west of Duluth, Minnesota) follows the shoreline of glacial Lake Minong and offers a panoramic view of the city and harbor.

The 138-foot-high **Aerial Lift Bridge** (Duluth, Minnesota), which connects Canal Park with Minnesota Point, spans the ship canal built in 1871 to give freighters access to Duluth harbor. Built for automobile traffic, the bridge can be lifted in fifty-five seconds to allow a Great Lakes freighter to enter or leave the harbor.

Great Lakes Aquarium (Harbor Drive, Duluth, Minnesota) contains every species of fish found in the Great Lakes, as well as other aquatic animals.

Glensheen Historic Estate (London Road, Duluth, Minnesota) was built in 1908 by an iron range baron. The Jacobean-style mansion and twenty-two-acre estate is owned and operated by the University of Minnesota–Duluth. Its furnishings and landscaping convey the splendor of a millionaire's existence at the turn of the century.

The **Duluth and Iron Range Railroad Depot** (Two Harbors, Minnesota) houses the Lake County Historical Society's museum, which features locomotives and ore cars used to bring ore from the Mesabi Range to Two Harbors.

sawmilling center, though it lagged well behind Minneapolis, Stillwater, and Winona. More significant was the shipment of grain out of Duluth, beginning with the first major dock elevator built in 1871 and surpassing sawmill operations through the 1890s.

In the late 1870s the Northern Pacific Railroad completed a spur line from Duluth to Brainerd, where it met the railroad's main line that fed westward into the wheat-growing Red River Valley. Duluth became (and remains today) a major shipping port for western wheat. Steamship companies developed a highly lucrative trade carrying grain to Lake Erie ports and returning with coal from Ohio's bituminous fields. With a population of thirty-three thousand in 1890, Duluth was Lake Superior's largest port. Only belatedly did it become an ore port, even though the richest iron ore beds in North America lay just sixty miles to the northwest. When the first ore was shipped out of the Vermilion Range in 1884, it went not to Duluth but to Agate Bay some thirty miles to the east on Minnesota's North Shore, soon to become the new lake port of Two Harbors.

In the mid-1870s, geological surveyors working the old Indian trail between the St. Louis River and Lake Vermilion in far northern Minnesota discovered a huge bed of iron rock near the lake. They returned with news of the iron and samples of "gold." Their samples turned out to be iron pyrite, "fool's gold," and a mini–gold rush quickly evaporated. Duluth founder George Stuntz suspected there was more to the story. He made his own trek to Lake Vermilion, found the thick outcropping of iron the surveyors had mentioned, and became convinced it was another iron deposit as rich in potential as were the Gogebic and Marquette ranges to the east. He brought back samples and showed them to his friend, Duluth merchant George C. Stone. The pair obtained some eastern financing and in 1882 formed the Minnesota Iron Company. The company purchased twenty thousand acres of logged-out land on the Vermilion Range, and Stone, a member of the Minnesota legislature, obtained a land grant to build a railroad from the range to Lake Superior.

Stuntz, who listed surveying among his several callings, carved out the route. Although the railroad was named the Duluth and Iron Range, Stuntz chose Agate Bay for its lake terminal because it was closer to the ore deposits. As in the Gogebic and Marquette ranges, the ore was in the form of hard rock and had to be mined with drill, shovel, and black powder. While the railroad was under construction, Stuntz (now a mining engineer) led a crew of Michigan émigrés to open the Soudan Mine overlooking Lake Vermilion. In Two Harbors the company built an ore dock, the largest yet constructed on Superior, and brought in by scow a locomotive, the *Three Spot*, which is still on display at the city's historical museum. On June 30, 1884, the *Three Spot* pulled a train of ten ore-bearing cars onto the loading dock at Two Harbors, and an industry was born that continues today.

Iron was extracted by hand drill in Michigan's Jackson Mine
as well as in other mines on ranges in the Lake Superior region.

Stuntz's Duluth and Iron Range Railroad ran across the eastern end of the Mesabi Range, which contained the largest concentration of iron ore yet discovered anywhere in the world. The railroad builders failed to see the ore, however, because it lay under glacial drift up to a hundred feet deep. In the 1870s Lewis H. Merritt, a Duluth founder and timber surveyor, picked up specimens of iron ore when he traversed the Mesabi looking for white pine, but he died before he could confirm his discovery. He passed his intuition on to his sons, who became known in Minnesota lore as the "Seven Iron Men." In 1889 the Merritt brothers dug some experimental pits on the Mesabi and uncovered heavy reddish earth. It had the color and weight of iron ore, but it was so loose it could be picked up by a shovel. All earlier finds, dating back to the Marquette Range, involved ore in the form of hard rock. The Merritts' discovery failed to arouse much interest because the mining community assumed eastern blast furnaces could not handle soft earth.

Lacking capital, the Merritts persuaded the Minnesota legislature to lease the range land on the same basis that it had leased timber properties. The Merritts thus leased nearly twenty-three thousand acres of the Mesabi Range for a mere sixty-two cents an acre. Then, capitalizing on the rivalry between Duluth and Two Harbors, the Merritt brothers persuaded several Duluth businessmen to help finance a railroad line from the Mesabi to the Duluth harbor.

At that point John D. Rockefeller entered the picture. Anxious to diversify the Standard Oil Company's assets, Rockefeller had purchased the Minnesota Iron Company's holdings on the Vermilion Range in 1887. In 1892, at Rockefeller's urging, steel magnate Andrew Carnegie offered the Merritts eight million dollars for their leased lands and railroad, but the "Seven Iron Men" turned him down. Although they were living high and splashing money all over Duluth, the Merritts nevertheless needed capital to improve their railroad facilities and ore dock. Using intermediaries to disguise his interest, Rockefeller extended them loans eventually totaling $1.6 million. When the panic of 1893 struck, bringing on a prolonged depression, the Merritts were unable to pay off the debt. In a complicated and protracted series of financial deals, Rockefeller ended up with the mining properties on the Mesabi, the railroad, and the ore docks. In 1901, when Andrew Carnegie and financier

At the turn of the century, steamers like the *North West* plied Lake Superior
filled with excursionists eager to visit points of interest ranging from
Pictured Rocks to bustling port cities.

J. P. Morgan organized the U.S. Steel Corporation, Rockefeller sold his
Minnesota mining interests to the new billion-dollar holding company.

Although Duluth retained, and over the years expanded, its ore dock,
it remained primarily a lumber and grain lake port. By 1907 its annual
tonnage in lumber, grain, and ore exceeded the shipping tonnage of
New York City.

Another of Duluth's major industries by the 1890s was tourism. Lake
freighters had carried passengers since the immigrant era of the 1830s,
but the first steamship built exclusively for travelers did not appear until
1894. It was the *North West*, the first of two great steel liners built by the

Great Northern Railroad to run between Buffalo and Duluth. The vessel had 178 staterooms capable of housing four hundred passengers. It stood as high above the water as a two-story building and could travel at twenty-two miles an hour. Its kitchen had a massive refrigerator, and its grand saloon was lined with rich mahogany and offered grandly stuffed and upholstered furniture. The excursion rate from Duluth to New York City, by way of the lakes and the Erie Canal, was $27.50 round-trip. After the turn of the century, thanks to competition from the railroads, the great passenger liners on the lake were used more for tourist excursions than for long-distance travel. Ship passenger service peaked in 1902 when 121,292 travelers passed through the port. By then, Duluth's railroad stations (each railroad maintained its own depot) were handling fifty passenger trains a day.

The Heyday of Commercial Fishing

In the year 1872 a half-million tons of iron ore passed through the Sault canal, along with some fifteen thousand tons of copper and a half-million bushels of wheat. What is striking about these figures is the absence of lumber. The 1870s ushered in lumbering to the piney woods of northern Wisconsin and Minnesota, but the lumbering frontier had not really reached Lake Superior. The lake was surrounded by dense forests, but its cool and foggy climate was better suited to spruce, hemlock, and balsam fir than to white pine. The sparse white and red pine lumbered in the lake's watershed went into housing construction in the booming cities of Marquette, Houghton, Hancock, Hurley, and Ironwood. Railroads would eventually tap the pinelands of northern Minnesota and carry the logs into Duluth, but not until late in the century. Duluth's first shipment of sawn lumber by lake steamship occurred in 1881.

Another surprise, besides the absence of lumber from the list of traffic through the Sault canal in 1872, is the presence of 576,000 half barrels of fish. That figure was more than twice the production of the previous year and signaled the rebirth of an industry that had died in infancy in the 1840s. Three developments in that thirty-year interval spurred the resurrection. A surge of Irish and German immigrants fleeing the European potato famine brought into the farms and cities of the Middle

West a largely Catholic population whose religion demanded a weekly fasting on fish. The American Fur Company's experiment with commercial fishing in the 1830s had failed in part for lack of a market; by the end of the Civil War demand existed. A second immigration surge in the post–Civil War decades brought large numbers of Scandinavians to American shores. Swedish and Norwegian fishing folk migrated to Lake Superior in hopes of pursuing their craft. They settled in Ashland and Duluth and founded fishing communities along Minnesota's North Shore and on Isle Royale. The nascent fishing industry now had a skilled force accustomed to hard work and meager returns. The third factor in the revival of commercial fishing on Lake Superior was the appearance of wholesale fish dealers who could organize the independent fishermen and deliver their products to market. The most important dealer, labeled the "Fishery Trust" by the *New York Times,* was A. Booth and Company of Chicago.

Born in England, Alfred Booth moved to Chicago in 1848 at age twenty. He opened a small store trading in fish and vegetables and personally matched Chicago's growth. By 1870 his mercantile firm was rated commercially in the $100,000 to $250,000 range. During the 1870s he opened fish warehouses in various ports on Lake Michigan, and by the following decade he was ready to conquer Lake Superior. His attention first fell on Bayfield, a fishing village on Chequamegon Bay, when the Chicago, St. Paul, Minneapolis and Omaha Railroad completed a line to the community in 1883.

Bayfield, on the western shore of Chequamegon Bay opposite Madeline Island, had been founded in 1856, about the same time as Ashland and Superior. Although its developers, a group of bankers from Washington, DC, initially hoped to make it an ore port, the lack of copper in the vicinity and the absence of any immediate prospect of obtaining a railroad forced them to think of tourism. Within a year they had built a hotel and founded a newspaper. The main function of the paper was to tout the advantages of Bayfield over Ashland and Superior as a railroad terminus and commercial entrepôt. By 1860 it had a population of 353.

Bayfield, like Ashland and Superior, lost population during the Civil War, but it remained a viable community, supported by small-scale fishing and tourism. A state census of 1865 indicated a population of about 250, and its hotels had become famous for their whitefish dinners (and remain so today). In 1870 fishing families from Minnesota's North Shore established the first commercial fishery in Bayfield. They brought with them Mackinaw boats to set nets around the Apostle Islands and a schooner to carry their barrels of fish to market. The village's two saw-mills, previously specializing in cedar shingles, began making barrel staves to accommodate the fishermen.

The success of Bayfield's fishing operation attracted the attention of the A. Booth Company in 1883. The company built a warehouse and sent small steamers to collect the catch of independent fishermen liv-ing on inlets along the south shore of the lake. By 1885 Booth and three

PORT CITIES

Located at the head of the Lakes and blessed with "one of the finest natu-ral harbors in the world," **Duluth-Superior** has long been an important grain, timber, and iron ore exporter. Today, the Duluth-Superior area comprises the largest metropolitan site on the lake. Duluth stars as an employer in the medical field, and its educational institutions contribute to its place as a freshwater research site. Superior competes as a trans-portation center—its Burlington Northern Santa Fe ore docks are the largest in the world—and continues to construct ships on the water-front. For the Twin Ports, tourism is a major industry, as visitors come to play along the lake and to take advantage of bountiful cultural and outdoor opportunities.

From fur to trade goods to silver to pulp and paper production, **Thunder Bay**—created in 1970 from the merger of Fort William and Port Arthur—has embraced various industries along the way to becoming the largest outbound port on the St. Lawrence Seaway System, greeting more than 400 ships annually. Today the city of nearly 110,000—the largest on the Lake Superior Circle Tour—supplies regional markets and offers services and culture to visitors and locals from its central Canadian location.

The Lake Superior Fish Company was one of many concerns that carted crates of fish from dock to city market in the early twentieth century.

other dealers in Bayfield employed "several hundred men nearly all year around," according to the *Bayfield County Press*. The harvest sent to eastern markets that year totaled 2.5 million pounds. Unfortunately, the whitefish, an abundant food source to Indians fishing from canoes, proved too vulnerable to commercial net fishing. By 1894 the catch in Bayfield was so poor that Booth employed a single tug to collect the harvest of Lake Superior's south shore.

By the 1890s the Booth Company controlled the marketing of most of the fish caught in both the American and Canadian waters of Lake Superior. Besides Bayfield, it had packinghouses in Sault Ste. Marie, Duluth, and Port Arthur, Ontario. On the Canadian side of the lake, Booth's agent at Sault Ste. Marie furnished fishermen with rods and nets. Because of the equipment used, the fish were considered American under American customs laws, even though the fishermen worked under Canadian licenses. As a result, Booth's barrels of Canadian fish entered the United States duty free.

When whitefish became scarce on the lake's south shore, the Booth Company opened a branch in Port Arthur on Thunder Bay, across the river from old Fort William. It employed about fifteen Canadians operating from two tugs and three sailboats to net whitefish. Booth also purchased the harvest of independent Canadian fishermen operating as far away as Nipigon Bay. The Booth steamer *Dixon* carried most of the Port Arthur catch to Duluth, from whence they were sent to Chicago as American fish.

Until the gasoline engine came into use after World War I, the standard fishing craft was the Mackinaw boat. Although the term originally referred to any small craft that carried both oars and sails, including the flat-bottomed French bateau, by the mid-nineteenth century the term was attached to a specific boat design: a round-bottomed craft, pointed both fore and aft. The design was influenced by Scandinavian immigrants who fished from similar craft in both the Baltic and the North Atlantic. The bow was shear and high to slice through waves in rough seas. The stern was similarly sheared in order to handle waves in a following sea. The round bottom—and often a centerboard keel—made for swift sailing. Mackinaws averaged eighteen to twenty-six feet in length and six to eight feet abeam. They had two stubby masts—stability being more important than speed—and schooner-rigged sails. Small enough to be rowed when the wind was either too strong or nonexistent, they were also light enough to be beached in a storm.

The best season for fishing was the autumn. Trout and whitefish came into shallow waters in early fall and spawned in October and November. Both species, which averaged two to three feet in size, were caught in gill nets. These highly effective tools functioned like an underwater fence, anchored to the bottom in shallow water and held on the surface by floats. They were made of fine string woven into a coarse mesh. The fish swam unseeingly into the net and became trapped, their gills preventing them from escaping backward. In 1894 a fisherman boasted of having taken a thousand pounds of trout from an eight-hundred-foot-long gill net on a spawning reef halfway between Duluth and Split Rock.

A fisherman checks and repairs his nets before heading out for the next catch.

After whitefish nearly disappeared in the 1890s, lake trout became commercial fishermen's favorite quarry. In addition to the spawning season, they could be caught in the spring by hook and line. From April till June the trout were widely dispersed and swam at varying depths, depending on water temperature and their prey's location. Fishermen trolled from their Mackinaw boats using a "main line" of linen thread one-eighth of an inch thick. The main line carried forty hooks spaced sixty feet apart. From each hook was hung a baited "snell hook" at depths ranging from 48 to 180 feet. The rig thus attracted fish swimming at various depths as it was dragged across the fishing grounds. Hook and line fishermen preferred a rough sea because the waves caused more "action" on the baited hooks. Trout production on Lake Superior rose from 1.6 million pounds in 1879 to 5.8 million in 1899.

From the 1880s through the first decade of the twentieth century, the American and Canadian governments made periodic attempts to negotiate a treaty that would limit harvests on all the Great Lakes and preserve threatened species. They achieved nothing, however, largely due to the political clout of great marketing combines like A. Booth Company. By the turn of the century, fishermen were turning to species previously scorned, notably herring. These creatures, averaging only about a pound in weight, had previously been caught mainly for bait. Fishermen ate them in hard times or sold them to the poor. During the 1890s, fish processors discovered ways of pickling and smoking herring that made them quite tasty, but they never approached the market value of trout or whitefish. The Scandinavians of Isle Royale and Minnesota's North Shore, acquainted with herring in the Old Country, were the most productive of herring fishermen.

VISITING HISTORY

The **Bayfield Maritime Museum** (South First Street, Bayfield, Wisconsin) focuses on Bayfield's commercial fishing and boat-building traditions.

Hokenson Fishery (off Highway 13, about twelve miles north of Bayfield, Wisconsin) contains the dock and storage sheds of a family-owned fishery dating from the 1920s.

Edison Fishery (Rock Harbor, Isle Royale National Park) hosts exhibits on commercial fishing on Isle Royale.

The **North Shore Commercial Fishing Museum** (Highway 61, Tofte, Minnesota) features displays on the lives of fishermen, the boats they used, and the techniques of the catch.

Between 1900 and 1940, the United States and Canada shipped one-third of the world's grain, and the Duluth-Superior harbor handled nearly 20 percent of all grain shipped on the upper Great Lakes. Here, grain is loaded on a freighter at the Great Northern elevator in Superior, 1940.

The herring came into shallow water in the autumn to spawn, and they were caught in pound nets. The pound net, held up by stakes pounded into the lake bottom, consisted of a mesh net "leader," five to fourteen hundred feet long, that guided fish into a heart-shaped enclosure that, in turn, channeled them through a tunnel into the net's pot. The pot was a twenty- to forty-foot-square enclosure from which the fisherman scooped the catch into a round-bottom skiff. The typical North Shore–Isle Royale skiff was sixteen feet long with pointed bow and stern.

Propelled by oars, it could be handled by a single fisherman. When his boat was full, the fisherman rowed his catch to the pier and transferred the fish into boxes. Not trusting the honesty of the warehouseman, he carefully weighed each box. He then stored the fish in ice until the Booth Company steamer made its rounds. Because the steamer was often unable to enter the shallow bays of Isle Royale, the fisherman sometimes had to meet the steamer out in the lake to transfer his boxes and receive payment.

Although the annual catch of lake trout and herring declined slowly but steadily after 1900, good prices kept the number of fishermen fairly stable. There is no census of the lake's total fishing population, but figures from Isle Royale are probably representative: there were about 135 fishing families on the island in 1890 and about 115 in 1925. Completion of the North Shore road from Duluth to Grand Portage in 1924 helped break the Booth Company's monopoly in western Lake Superior. North Shore and Isle Royale fishermen could bring their boxes of iced fish into Grand Marais or Grand Portage and meet independent truckers who carried the harvest to market. In Port Arthur, Duluth, and Sault Ste. Marie, the development of marketing cooperatives also helped break the Booth monopoly. Competitive pricing and governmental fish hatcheries promised a bright future for Lake Superior fishermen.

Then disaster struck. Construction of the Welland Ship Canal, connecting lakes Ontario and Erie and bypassing Niagara Falls, dated to 1829. When enlarged in 1932, it opened the Great Lakes to the ocean-going traffic of the St. Lawrence. Along with oceanic freighters came a saltwater alien, the sea lamprey. This parasitic bloodsucker attached itself to large fish, especially trout and whitefish, and eventually killed them. It reached Lake Superior sometime around 1930 and destroyed the commercial fishing industry. But the struggle with and ultimate victory over the sea lamprey is a story for another chapter.

CHAPTER SIX

LIGHTHOUSES AND SHIPWRECKS

SINCE 1816, when the North West Company's fur-trading schooner *Invincible* foundered in a gale on Whitefish Point, about 550 shipwrecks have been recorded on Lake Superior. The wrecks were not evenly distributed around the lake, however. The majority occurred in two famous "graveyards": the Michigan shore from Whitefish Point west to Copper Harbor and at Isle Royale.

Michigan's "shipwreck coast" took a greater toll than any other part of the lake for several reasons. Whitefish Point, together with its mate on the Canadian side, Iroquois Point, forms the entrance to Whitefish Bay which, in turn, channels shipping into Sault Ste. Marie. Nearly all lake traffic must pass through this funnel, lines of downbound (easterly) vessels passing lines of upbound (westerly) ones. Despite designated traffic lanes, collisions occurred even under good weather conditions. Impaired visibility due to snow, smoke from forest fires, or the infamous Lake Superior fog increased the chances of collision or grounding.

Another reason for the carnage on the Upper Peninsula shoreline was the grand sweep of water for the buildup of storms. The worst of Lake Superior's storms came out of the northwest; with free passage of 160 miles from Thunder Bay to Whitefish Point, a gale-force wind could whip up waves over thirty feet high. Even a storm of modest force crashing into the stern of a downbound vessel could take out the steering mechanism, leaving the ship, whether sailing vessel or steamer, to drift helplessly onto the Michigan shore.

Isle Royale was another "graveyard" for ships on Lake Superior. Since 1840, when the American Fur Company's schooner *Siskawit* foundered on a rock while entering Siskiwit Bay on the island's east side, Isle Royale has claimed about a dozen vessels. Ten major wrecks, steel-hulled steamships, lying within Isle Royale National Park have been located, identified, and explored. The island, forty-five miles long and nine miles wide, is surrounded by several hundred islets, rocky outcrops, and underwater reefs. It sits astride the two major shipping lanes of the western part of the lake, one running to Thunder Bay, the other to Duluth–Superior–Two Harbors. A mere twenty miles from Ontario's rocky shore, it also created a perilously narrow passage for traffic between Port Arthur/Fort William and Duluth.

VISITING HISTORY

Dating from 1849, **Copper Harbor Lighthouse** (Copper Harbor, Michigan) and the light at Whitefish Point are the oldest on the lake. The keeper's house is a museum depicting the life of a light keeper and his family. Not accessible to visitors by land, the light can be reached via a small passenger ferry from the Municipal Marina.

Automated since 1970, **Whitefish Point Lighthouse** (Whitefish Point Road, eleven miles north of Paradise, Michigan) provides light, fog signal, and radio beacons for ships bound to or from the Sault Ste. Marie canal.

Split Rock Lighthouse (Highway 61, north of Two Harbors, Minnesota) is the most frequently visited lighthouse on the lake. The entire light station, with an adjacent interpretive center, is now a state historic site operated by the Minnesota Historical Society and surrounded by 2,200-acre Split Rock Lighthouse State Park.

Rock Harbor Light (Isle Royale) was built in 1855 to guide copper ore boats and has since been restored by the National Park Service.

Given the hazards presented by Whitefish Point and Isle Royale, it is scarcely surprising that authorities in Michigan and Wisconsin were demanding federally financed lighthouses even before the Sault canal was built and steamships invaded the lake.

The U.S. Lighthouse Service

From 1716—when colonial Boston installed the first American light-house—to 1789, each colony and state assumed responsibility for erecting and maintaining lighthouses within their boundaries. In the latter year, the First Congress passed an act giving the federal government control of all aids to interstate and international navigation, although a Lighthouse Service was not formally created until 1820. Even then Congress placed the service under the indifferent management of a minor functionary of the Treasury Department. The service finally installed lights on Lake Superior at Whitefish Point and Copper Harbor in 1847, but dissatisfaction with the service's management led Congress in 1852 to approve a plan for a nine-member Lighthouse Board chaired by the Secretary of the Treasury. (The Department of Commerce was not established until 1903.) The board divided the country into twelve Lighthouse Districts. A district inspector was charged with the construction of lighthouses "and with the purchase, the setting up, and the repairs of the illuminating apparatus."

So far as Lake Superior was concerned, the Lighthouse Board was not much more effective than the previous management. It did build a light-house at Rock Harbor near the northeast tip of Isle Royale in 1855 but discontinued it four years later when copper mining on the island ceased. The board apparently felt that the safety of shipping bound for Thunder Bay was a problem for the Canadians. Not until 1867 did the Lighthouse Board become concerned that there was no light on Michigan's "shipwreck coast" between Whitefish Point and Copper Harbor. Despite annual requests from the board, Congress until 1872 delayed appropriating funds for a light at "Big Sable," actually Au Sable Point. The state of Michigan obligingly designated a 326-acre tract on the point as "swampland" and conveyed it without charge to the Treasury Department. The facility was completed in 1874 and, electrified in the 1920s, remains in operation today.

Hazardous Isle Royale was next to win the Lighthouse Board's attention. In 1875 the board built a light tower and keepers' quarters on Menagerie Island, near the middle of the eastern side of the island at the entrance to Siskiwit Bay. That same year it obtained a congressional appropriation to establish a lighthouse on Passage Island, some three miles off the northeastern point of Isle Royale. Because the light would chiefly benefit the growing grain trade out of Port Arthur, Congress imposed a condition that the Dominion of Canada install a light on its side of the Detroit River. Construction was delayed for five years while the Canadians found money and made plans for their light. The Passage Island lamp was finally illuminated on July 1, 1882. Along with the light, the board installed a coal-fired steam foghorn. In its first season of use (May to November), the fog signal ran for 174 hours, an indication of the frequency with which a shroud of white vapor descends upon the lake.

Also in 1882, the Lighthouse Board completed construction of a light tower on Stannard Rock, a largely underwater reef whose glacially rounded surface poked only a few feet above water level. Lying twenty-four miles off the Keweenaw Peninsula on a direct line between its tip and Whitefish Point, this "loneliest piece of real estate in the United States" was without doubt the deadliest single hazard to lake traffic. First spotted in 1835 by Captain C. C. Stannard, who was taking the American Fur Company's *John Jacob Astor* on its maiden voyage, the rock was so obscure that he initially thought it merely a capsized bateau.

Construction of a beacon on the rock was a major undertaking since much of the reef was underwater. Engineers first had to install a cofferdam to keep the lake waters at bay while they built a stone and concrete base, ninety-eight feet in diameter and extending fifteen feet below the lake surface and twenty-two feet above it. From Lake Erie, barges brought smooth granite blocks to form the lighthouse tower. Engineers stacked the blocks on the shore as a rehearsal for the difficult construction to come. They then dismantled the shoreline edition, carefully numbering each block to speed final construction. It took five years to complete the structure at a cost of three hundred thousand dollars, four times the average price tag for a lighthouse in that day. The tower rose 110 feet above the water, and its light was visible for thirty or forty miles on a clear night. Since there was no room on the base for a house, the keeper

Like many lighthouses, the one on Isle Royale included a light tower and house for the light keeper and his family. The foghorn stood in a separate building.

had to make do with cramped quarters within the tower. Supplies were initially brought by sailboat from Marquette, but because of the shoals the cartons had to be transferred to the keeper's rowboat for landing on the base. In later years the keeper was furnished with a twenty-five-foot motor launch for trips to Marquette. Because the lake would have swept away any sort of dock, the launch had to be lifted onto the lighthouse deck by crane at the end of each journey. The Stannard Rock Lighthouse is today fully automated and unmanned.

Among the dozens of lighthouses built on Lake Superior in the next half century, two more rate special attention: Rock of Ages Lighthouse off the southwestern tip of Isle Royale and Split Rock Lighthouse on the cliffs of Minnesota's North Shore near Silver Bay. Until the North Shore highway (U.S. 61) was completed in the 1920s, the only route for freight and passengers between Port Arthur/Fort William and Duluth/Superior was by water. The two lighthouses helped guide vessels through the narrow passage between Isle Royale and the North Shore. The Split Rock Lighthouse, in addition, was a beacon for ore boats emerging from Duluth, Superior, and Two Harbors.

The Lighthouse Board's attention was first drawn to the problem of the Isle Royale passage by the 1877 loss of the side-wheel steamer *Cumberland* on the Rock of Ages reef, which poked only a few feet above the water some three miles from Washington Harbor on the island's southwestern tip. With customary lethargy the board did not actually request an appropriation until 1895, and Congress dawdled for another ten years. In the meantime, in 1898 another large steamship, the *Henry Chisholm,* collided with the reef and sank in shallow water nearby. With a congressional appropriation at last, construction began on a steel cylindrical base in 1907, and a hundred-foot tower was completed the following year. Congress was less dilatory with appropriations for Split Rock Lighthouse on the Minnesota shore, probably because of pressure from U.S. Steel and other iron ore companies. A brick tower and keeper's house were completed in 1910, and, though no longer in use as a beacon, today the structure is in the National Register of Historic Places and part of a Minnesota state park.

Keepers and Their Lights

Until the mid-nineteenth century, the lamp at the top of a lighthouse was a whale oil–burning wick backed by a parabolic lens that reflected the light into a beam. Although visible for only a few miles—and scarcely at all in a fog—its redeeming feature to a penurious Treasury Department was its low cost of operation. When the Lighthouse Board took charge in the 1850s, it recommended adoption of a much more effective lamp, invented by French physicist Augustin-Jean Fresnel. The Fresnel lens was essentially a glass barrel whose outer surface was a series of glass prisms and convex lenses that focused the light into a steady beam. The light source remained a wick lamp in the center. As whales became scarce in midcentury and the price of their oil rose, the board experimented with other fuels and ultimately settled on kerosene. In the early twentieth century, the board replaced the wick lamp in most Fresnel lenses with an oil-vapor lamp using an incandescent mantle. This innovation increased the light's intensity and hence its visibility by a factor of ten. In the 1920s, when new technology permitted electricity to be carried into rural areas, the board replaced the oil lamps with electric lights. This

The light at Stannard Rock, on the "loneliest piece of real estate in the United States," provides essential guidance to ship traffic off the Keweenaw Peninsula.

advance ultimately doomed the position of the lighthouse keeper, for his principal job was trimming the wick and cleaning the lens of soot.

The calling of lighthouse keeper was a lonely and monotonous one. Complained one keeper at the Au Sable light, "The trouble with our life here is that we have too much time to think!" Lighthouses were typically manned by two individuals: a keeper and his assistant—in many cases a man and wife team. The board's publication *Instructions to Light-Keepers* specified their duties and spelled out with bureaucratic precision every detail of life at the station. It required, for instance, that only "substantial and wholesome food . . . be provided at the station," a regulation presumably directed at the onshore suppliers. With characteristic penury,

This Fresnel lens served at Copper Harbor lighthouse.

the board's *Instructions* forbade servers from furnishing keepers with "articles known as luxurious."

The principal—indeed, almost the only—task of the keeper was to see that the light came on at sunset and burned brightly until dawn. The *Instructions* divided the workload into shifts. The first, lasting from sunset to midnight, was manned by the assistant and included trimming the wick and cleaning soot off the lens. The second, manned by the keeper, lasted from midnight until 10:00 in the morning (the *Instructions* directed that all tasks be completed by that hour); in addition to trimming the wick and cleaning soot, he was to polish the light's copper and brass fixtures. The *Instructions* were deeply concerned about dust or grit that might scratch the glass prisms. They required the keeper to wear an apron "made of suitable linen . . . to protect the apparatus from injury from contact of coarse clothing, metal buttons, etc." The keeper's final task, at 10:00 AM, was to have everything in order for lighting in the evening. When that was accomplished, he was to clothe the entire lantern in a linen curtain. This curtain was "not to be used for any other purposes," and under no circumstances was it "to be used in the keeper's dwelling."

Given the utter isolation of most lighthouses, one might suppose that these meticulous directives were honored, for the most part, in the breach. Not so: each of the Lighthouse Districts had an inspector, whose unannounced rounds were dreaded by every keeper. Failure to pass a military-style "white glove inspection" could result in demotion or dismissal from the service. Some inspectors rated a station by how well the keeper's wife maintained the living quarters. One confessed that if he found the cottage spotless, he would compliment the wife and suggest that she oversee her husband's work on the light; if he found the household disorderly, he would take the husband aside and recommend better masculine leadership. The level of domestic harmony left in his wake has mercifully gone unrecorded.

Some Legendary Wrecks

Steamboats entered Lake Superior even before the Sault canal was completed. Indeed, there were four on the lake by 1851, built on the lower lakes and dragged across the Sault portage. Each was equipped with

European-designed screw propellers rather than the side-wheels common on the eastern lakes and rivers. Because it pushed, rather than pulled, the boat through the water, the propeller could operate with a smaller engine placed farther aft, leaving more room for freight and passengers.

Although only four "propellers" serviced the lake in 1851, two of them, incredibly enough, collided. The victim was the 319-ton *Manhattan*, built in Cleveland in 1847 and portaged over the Sault the year before it sank. Another "propeller," the *Monticello*, rammed it when the two vessels confused signals while passing one another near Parisienne Island in the middle of Whitefish Bay. The *Manhattan* sank in shallow water that barely covered her decks, and apparently there was no loss of life. Nevertheless, a Methodist missionary aboard the *Monticello* could not forebear drawing a moral lesson. The passengers on the *Monticello*, he reported, had just consumed an oyster dinner and were dancing on the deck when the collision occurred. "Thus," he moralized, "are people often in the hight [*sic*] of conviviality, intoxicated by trifling amusement and sinful diversion . . ." when "there is but a step between them and death." Although the *Monticello* appeared to compensate for her moral transgression by helping to raise and repair the *Manhattan*, she wrecked only a month later on the west side of the Keweenaw.

The *Indiana* was another early "propeller" of similar size, 146 feet long and 23 feet in beam. Built on Lake Erie in 1847, she entered the Lake Superior trade after the Sault canal opened. On June 6, 1858, she departed Marquette with a load of iron ore in a nor'wester storm. The following sea apparently cracked her sternpost and ruptured a seal on the propeller shaft. She began to fill with water, and the twenty-one people aboard, passengers and crew, abandoned her in the ship's sail-rigged yawl. The survivors reached shore safely, insurance covered the twelve thousand dollar loss, and the *Indiana* was forgotten for the moment.

In 1972 divers discovered her resting on an even keel in 118 feet of water. Both the ship's wood and metal were well preserved. A consortium consisting of the Smithsonian Institution, the state of Michigan, the National Trust, the Army Corps of Engineers, and the Coast Guard recovered her eighteen-foot-high vertical steam engine, her ten-foot diameter iron propeller, her boiler, and other machine parts. Today these pieces are featured in the Smithsonian's National Museum of American

History. The *Indiana*'s machinery attracted public interest because it was forty years older than that recovered or preserved from any other American shipwreck. Its engine, according to the Smithsonian, "represents the earliest marine steam plant still in existence in North America which had an actual working history."

Late in the century, shipping companies began using freight-hauling sailing vessels as barges towed by steamships. The sails were merely auxiliary, and the towing or "consort" system doubled or tripled the steamer's per-trip capacity. On May 13, 1899, the steamer *A. Folsom* was towing the *Nelson*—a three-masted, 165-foot schooner built in Milwaukee in 1866—and another schooner-barge upbound for Hancock, Michigan, with a load of coal. After rounding Whitefish Point, they ran into a freezing northwest gale. The towline of the *Nelson* snapped in the heavy seas. Although the *Nelson*'s captain was able to set enough sail to hold her bow into the oncoming sea, her decks and rigging became coated with ice. When the vessel began to founder, the captain ordered his five-man crew, as well as his wife and daughter, into the schooner's yawl. The captain stayed aboard to man the davits that lowered the yawl into the water. With the yawl temporarily attached to the schooner by a bowline, the captain attempted to jump into the wildly pitching lifeboat. He missed and fell into the water. Surfacing, he watched in horror as the stern of the schooner pitched high into the air and the vessel quickly sank, dragging the yawl and its passengers to the bottom. Equipped with a life vest, the captain survived the freezing water and floated ashore near Grand Marais.

As tourism and passenger traffic expanded on the lake at the turn of the century, the chances for greater loss of life increased as well. The *Monarch,* built in 1890 at Sarnia, Ontario, at the foot of Lake Huron, was designed to carry a mix of passengers and packaged freight. Her wooden hull was timbered in white oak, and the passenger quarters exhibited the finest in materials and craftsmanship. A bit more than 240 feet in length, she was powered by a nine-hundred-horsepower steam engine.

The *Monarch* was making her last run of the season when she departed Port Arthur in the late afternoon of December 6, 1906, with twelve passengers and a mixed cargo of bagged grain, canned salmon, and cans of lead paint. After rounding Thunder Cape, her captain set a course for

Lake Superior has been the site of more than five hundred shipwrecks, including the *America*, which struck a reef off Isle Royale's Washington Harbor in 1928.

Passage Island off the tip of Isle Royale. Dense snow began to fall, and fog rose up from the water. Getting only an occasional glimpse of the Passage Island light, the captain calculated distance by his speed and time. Judging himself abreast of Passage Island, he set a new course for Whitefish Point. Moments later he plowed blindly into the palisades of Blake Point at Isle Royale's northeast tip. The bow was hung up on rocks, while the stern sank quickly to the shallow bottom. One crewman was thrown overboard, but the rest of the passengers and crew remained uninjured in the bow.

The crew launched a lifeboat, but the surf was too rough to permit a landing on the rocky shore. The boat was brought back aboard ship, and the crew devised a new strategy. With a rope they lowered a wooden ladder off the bow. Jack McCallum, who was working his passage to Sarnia as a deckhand, volunteered to descend to the bottom of the ladder. The crew then swung the ladder and McCallum pendulum fashion until he was close enough to the beach to leap ashore. Connected to the *Monarch* by a thin lifeline, McCallum worked his way to the top of the palisade and pulled up a length of heavy-duty rope from the vessel. He secured the rope to a tree, and one by one the crew clambered across to safety, hand over hand.

Safety proved relative, however, for the nearest settlement was miles away through trackless forest. For three nights and two days the crew huddled around bonfires and subsisted on what little they had carried off the ship in their pockets. On the third day the assistant keeper of the Passage Island light came across in a small boat to investigate the survivors' signal fire. The boat was too small to accommodate the crew, so the light keeper and a ship's officer sailed out into the traffic lane to flag down a passing freighter. They succeeded, and on December 10 a pair of tugboats from Port Arthur rescued the stranded sailors. The Canadian Board of Trade awarded Jack McCallum a medal for his gallant role in the rescue. The remnants of the *Monarch*'s hull can still be seen on the rocks of Blake Point.

Forecasting the weather on Lake Superior has always been chancy, for the moody sea could change from deceptive calm to pounding breakers in a matter of hours, even minutes. On November 8, 1913, an early winter snowstorm struck Lake Superior, and vessels waiting to make their last runs of the season prudently remained in port or took shelter behind Keweenaw or Whitefish points. The National Weather Bureau's forecast for the upper lakes the next day, however, was "unsettled" weather, and ship captains with schedules to meet set sail that morning. Undetected by the Weather Service was the birth of an intense cyclone on the Canadian plains. The storm descended on Lake Superior around noon on November 9, and the wind quickly built to a hurricane force of eighty miles an hour, with thirty-five-foot waves. The cyclonic winds swung from west to north to northeast, buffeting ships wherever they sought cover. Over the next three days the winds lashed beaches from Duluth to Chicago to Buffalo, wrecking forty vessels and taking 235 lives. It was the worst storm in Great Lakes' recorded history.

At midday on November 8 the *L. C. Waldo,* a modern steel ore boat, had departed Two Harbors with a load of iron ore. The storm caught the *Waldo* in the middle of the lake, and Captain Duddleson, a native of Sault Ste. Marie, steered for the shelter of Manitou Island, off the point of Keweenaw. By nightfall the pilothouse windows were caked with ice, and Captain Duddleson steered by compass and a guesswork reckoning of his speed. Around midnight a mountainous wave demolished the pilothouse. Duddleson and his wheelsman saved themselves by hanging onto a hatchway as the water poured over them. The main steering mechanism and the compass were disabled, as was the electric generator. Retrieving a portable compass from a lifeboat, captain and mate fought their way through the surf crashing over the deck to the forward deckhouse. With the mate holding a compass and lantern, the captain tried to steer for Manitou Island with an auxiliary wheel. He never made it. Within sight of the island's lighthouse, the *Waldo* went aground on a reef running out from Gull Rock.

Its hull resting amidships on the rocks, the vessel began to break apart. Captain Duddleson summoned the engine crew on deck. The crew inched forward on ropes to the forward deckhouse, carrying with them two terrified women and two gallon-size tins of tomatoes from the ship's galley. In all, twenty-nine people huddled in the deckhouse, the only dry place left on the ship, and there they remained for two nights and three days as the storm passed on to the southeast. The tomatoes, though monotonous fare, assuaged their hunger. For warmth they fashioned a stove out of the captain's bathtub, wrenched from its plumbing and turned upside down on bricks. They punched a hole in its bottom and formed a chimney out of a chain of emergency water pails with punched-out bottoms. They curved the stack of pails so the top one poked out a porthole, taking care of some, though by no means all, of the smoke. They built a fire on the steel deck under the bathtub, using furniture and wood paneling from the captain's quarters for fuel.

On November 12 a passing freighter spotted the wreck and notified the lifesaving stations at Eagle Harbor and Portage on the Keweenaw. Because of the raging seas, it was another half day before lifesaving crews in their "surfboats" rescued the *Waldo*'s stranded crew. The lifesavers' heroic effort in coming to the *Waldo*'s aid was only the latest in

In the days before high-tech weather forecasting, ships could be stranded by an early-season snowstorm, as was the City of Bangor in 1927 off Keweenaw Point.

the glorious history of a service that, like the Lighthouse Service, would ultimately become part of the U.S. Coast Guard.

The U.S. Life-Saving Service

In the 1850s the Treasury Department added lifesaving stations manned by volunteer crews to some lighthouses on the lower Great Lakes. The volunteers were inadequately trained and generally ineffective. As the number of shipwrecks on the lakes mounted, Congress in 1871 appropriated funds for a U.S. Life-Saving Service with permanent stations and paid crews. Four stations were built on Lake Superior in the mid-1870s, all of them on Michigan's "Shipwreck Coast," between Whitefish Point and Grand Marais. By the end of the century there were stations near every port on the lake and, where space permitted, every lighthouse was equipped with a lifesaving station.

Each station had a captain and eight surfmen. The government paid the captain an annual salary and required him to live at the station. The surfmen enlisted for the navigation season, April 15 to December 15, at sixty-five dollars a month. Most worked as lumberjacks in the wintertime. The government equipped each station with two types of boats—surfboats and lifeboats. The surfboat, twenty-five feet long and weighing about seven hundred pounds, could be launched from a beach. It was pointed at both ends, like the old bateau, and a weighted keel made it self-righting. Once a week the crew practiced a surfboat exercise: launching the boat, rowing it out through the breakers, capsizing it, righting it, and resuming rowing. The captain, who served as helmsman, was usually agile enough to squirm across the stern of the spinning boat without ever getting wet.

The lifeboat was considerably larger, measuring thirty to thirty-six feet in length and weighing nearly a ton. It, too, was pointed at both ends with a covered deck fore and aft. It was also self-righting, though the crew did not practice capsizing it. The lifeboat was housed in a shed on the beach and launched down a wooden ramp. Lifeboats were initially equipped with sails, but the government installed gasoline motors on them shortly after the turn of the century.

Before the arrival of radio, the lifesavers kept watch on the lake from lookout towers and twenty-four-hour beach patrols. When not on patrol or repairing equipment, the surfmen honed their skills with a Lyle gun on the beach. This piece of equipment was the primary means of rescue for vessels within six hundred yards of shore and when the seas were too rough to use a lifeboat. The Lyle gun, named for the army ordnance officer who invented it, was a small cannon that fired a seventeen-pound ball. Connected to the ball was a light line two inches in circumference that uncoiled from a box as the shot flew through the air. The entire apparatus, weighing a little more than half a ton, was hauled to a wreck scene in a two-wheel cart drawn by either the eight surfmen or a team of horses.

The beach drill with the Lyle gun began with the erection of a hundred-foot pole with crossbars, simulating a ship's mast. The crew practiced firing the cannon from various distances, attempting to get the cannonball close enough to the drill pole to wrap the light line around it. In a genuine wreck the surfmen would fire the cannon at the ship's mast, and sailors aboard the vessel would seize the line and pass it through a

This view of the Marquette Life-Saving Station in about 1900 shows both a surfboat (right) and a lifeboat, essential tools for the surfmen's important work.

pulley attached to the mast or some other sturdy piece of the ship. The light line was then used to pull a four-and-a-half-inch hawser between the ship and the beach. With pulleys at each end, the hawser became a traveling line on the same principle as a clothesline between urban apartment houses. The lifesaving crew would then attach a "breaches buoy" (consisting of a cork life buoy with canvas pants sewn on it) to the hawser, and one by one the stranded crew could be brought ashore.

The Treasury Department appended the Life-Saving Service to the U.S. Coast Guard in 1915, but its personnel, procedures, and equipment remained intact for several more years. Indeed, the most heroic rescue of its history occurred four years later, on November 14, 1919.

The *H. E. Runnels* was a 178-foot wooden steamer upbound for the Keweenaw with a load of coal when it ran into an early-winter nor'wester on Lake Superior. The captain, Hugh O'Hagen, prudently sought shelter in the Grand Marais harbor. The next morning, November 14, the winds seemed to have abated, and Captain O'Hagen resumed his journey to the Keweenaw. Shortly after he cleared Au Sable, the storm returned, and a sixty-mile-per-hour wind with blinding snow assaulted the *Runnels.* Captain O'Hagen ordered a return to Grand Marais, but the driving wind caused him to miss the entrance.

Surfman George Olson, atop the Grand Marais coast guard station lookout tower, spotted the *Runnels* and saw that it was on the wrong side of the harbor entrance. Although the steamer showed no distress signal, Olson alertly summoned the lifesaver crew, which launched the high-powered lifeboat but kept it at the dock behind the station. Because several of his crew were sick, lead surfman A. E. Kristopherson approached a coast guard cutter that had taken shelter in the harbor to ask for help. A guest on the coast guard vessel, John O. Anderson, a veteran of the Chicago lifesaving station, volunteered.

In the meantime, Captain O'Hagen tried to work the *Runnels* back into the lake for another run at the harbor. In the process, the rudder controls broke and the gale winds blew the *Runnels* onto a sandbar, some five hundred feet from shore. At the station the lifesaving crew got the lifeboat's engine started, but then it quit, for the moment irreparable. Under Anderson and Kristopherson's direction, the lifesaving crew and some coast guard sailors hauled the beach apparatus, which included a Lyle gun, down to the beach opposite the stranded *Runnels,* barely visible through the driving snow. The wooden vessel was beginning to break up under the driving surf, and it was only a matter of time before Captain O'Hagen and his crew of sixteen would drown.

Anderson calmly assembled the cannon, took aim at the ship—which was at the limit of the gun's range—allowed for windage, and fired. The cannonball neatly dropped the messenger line right across the ship's bow. The crew fastened the line to the wheelhouse, but they were unable to bring the four-inch hawser aboard because of the wind and waves, negating any rescue through the use of a breaches buoy. Anderson then devised an alternate plan. His coast guardsmen placed the disabled lifeboat under the messenger line that connected shore to ship and rigged lines from the bow and stern to the overhead line in trolley fashion.

Anderson and the surfmen rowed the lifeboat, held to its course by the ropes, out to the *Runnels*. When they reached the stricken vessel, however, the storm prevented them from passing a lifeline aboard. After some discussion, Anderson managed to persuade the sailors to come down the whip line hand over hand into the boat. Four had done so when Anderson noticed that the lifeboat crew was utterly exhausted and suffering from exposure. He returned to the beach and obtained a replacement crew. Anderson made three more trips out to the *Runnels*, and the last one was the most difficult of all. He had exhausted the supply of surfmen and sailors on the beach and had begun to employ as rowers volunteers from the city. On the fourth and last trip, he had only six—rather than eight—rowers.

Left on the *Runnels* were only two men, Captain O'Hagen and his first mate. Seeing that both were cold and worn, Anderson had them tie an extra line around their waists before attempting the hand-over-hand transfer to the lifeboat. It was well that he did so, for both men fell into the water and had to be pulled aboard the lifeboat. As the mate, who weighed three hundred pounds, came over the gunwale, the boat began shipping water, and three of the crew, including Anderson, fell into the lake. All aboard at last, everyone reached the shore safely. The U.S. Treasury Department awarded all participants in this heroic rescue its highest honor, the Gold Lifesaving Medal.

Wreck of the *Edmund Fitzgerald*

Technological advances in the mid-twentieth century rendered Lake Superior's lighthouse keepers and lifesaving crews superfluous. Modern lake vessels are large enough and equipped with engines powerful enough to withstand the angriest of storms. No longer accustomed to taking shelter in a storm, captains plot travel routes down the center of the lake, usually beyond the reach of land-based stations and lighthouses. The few remaining lighthouses have automatic electric lights powered by solar batteries. Helicopters have replaced the lifesaving crews and their surfboats. Nonetheless, all of this advanced technology failed to prevent the greatest shipwreck of them all, the *Edmund Fitzgerald*. The *Fitzgerald*'s sinking is also the lake's greatest mystery.

The **Great Lakes Shipwreck Museum** (eleven miles north of Paradise, Michigan) is the only museum that focuses almost exclusively on Great Lakes maritime disasters. The site includes a restored coast guard life-boat station.

The **Grand Marais Maritime Museum and Light Keepers Museum** (Pictured Rocks National Lakeshore, Grand Marais, Michigan) contains exhibits of shipwrecks and the work of the U.S. Lifesaving Service. The nearby Light Keepers Museum is furnished as the living quarters of a light keeper and his family.

Named for the president of the Northwestern Mutual Life Insurance Company, the *Edmund Fitzgerald* was a 729-foot ore boat launched at River Rouge, Michigan, in 1958. Until 1971 the *Fitzgerald* was the largest vessel on the Great Lakes. Between bow and stern she had twenty-one separate cargo hatches for the loading and unloading of coal and ore.

The *Fitzgerald* departed Superior on the afternoon of November 9, 1975, with a load of twenty-seven thousand tons of iron ore. Off Two Harbors she met another ore boat, the *Arthur M. Anderson,* which fell in about ten miles behind the *Fitzgerald,* and the two vessels continued on a northeastward course. During the evening they received gale warnings by radio, and the captains chose to follow the north shore of the lake for protection. During the night the winds rose to over fifty knots from the northeast, and waves were running at twelve feet. At midmorning on the tenth of November, the vessels changed course to the southeast to bring them into the Soo (the modern colloquial spelling of the French *Sault*). The winds abated in midday but rose again in the afternoon after shifting to the northwest.

With the seas coming in from the starboard quarter, the *Anderson's* captain, Bernie Cooper, noted that his decks were awash with sixteen-foot waves. At 3:30 PM the *Fitzgerald* reported by radio that she was taking on

The *Edmund Fitzgerald*, which would become Lake Superior's
most infamous wreck, departs Duluth-Superior.

water and had begun to list. A half hour later the *Fitzgerald* spoke to a
passing upbound vessel: the radioman reported that he had a "bad list,
lost both radars, and was taking heavy seas over his decks." About that
time the Soo locks closed after reporting ninety-mile-per-hour wind
gusts. At 7:10 PM, when the *Fitzgerald* was about seventeen miles from
Whitefish Point and shelter, the pilothouse crew made their last radio
call to the *Anderson,* reporting that the *Fitzgerald* was taking on water
but the pumps were working and "they were holding their own." Minutes
later the *Fitzgerald* disappeared from the *Anderson*'s radar screen. She

went down so fast that no one in her crew even had time to pick up the radio microphone.

The coast guard undertook a massive search for the vessel by air and sea, but all it found over the next three days were some damaged lifeboats and scattered life jackets on the Ontario shore. On November 14 a navy antisubmarine aircraft located the *Fitzgerald*'s hull at the exact spot that it had disappeared from the *Anderson*'s screen. A sonar search placed the depth at 556 feet. The following spring the coast guard used a remote-controlled underwater recovery vehicle to examine the wreck. The device determined that the *Fitzgerald* had broken into three parts. The bow sat upright on the floor of the lake, while the stern lay upside down some distance away. The middle third was nothing but crushed and shattered hull fragments, buried in mud.

After looking at videotape footage taken by underwater cameras, the coast guard and the National Transportation Safety Board concluded that the hatch covers had failed, allowing water into the hold that caused the initial list. The heavy seas then caused the hatch covers to collapse, sinking the ship instantly. The two agencies disagreed as to whether the hatch covers had been inadequately fastened when the vessel departed Superior or whether they were inherently faulty. Likely only the insurance companies cared. The *Fitzgerald*'s crew of twenty-nine remain today in their watery grave.

Songwriter Gordon Lightfoot offered an epitaph in his ballad "The Wreck of the *Edmund Fitzgerald*," which made it to number two on the 1976 popular music charts.

> The legend lives on from the Chippewa on down
> of the big lake they called "Gitche Gumee."
> The lake, it is said, never gives up her dead
> when the skies of November turn gloomy.
> With a load of iron ore—twenty-six thousand tons more
> than the *Edmund Fitzgerald* weighed empty,
> that good ship and true was a bone to be chewed
> when the "Gales of November" came early.
>
> The ship was the pride of the American side
> coming back from some mill in Wisconsin.
> As the big freighters go, it was bigger than most
> with a crew and good captain well seasoned,
> concluding some terms with a couple of steel firms
> when they left fully loaded for Cleveland.
> And later that night when the ship's bell rang,
> could it be the north wind they'd been feelin'?
>
> The wind in the wires made a tattle-tale sound
> and a wave broke over the railing.
> And ev'ry man knew, as the captain did too
> 'twas the witch of November come stealin'.
> The dawn came late and the breakfast had to wait
> when the Gales of November came slashin'.
> When afternoon came it was freezin' rain
> in the face of a hurricane west wind.
>
> When suppertime came the old cook came on deck saying
> "Fellas, it's too rough t'feed ya."

At 7 PM a main hatchway caved in; he said
"Fellas, it's bin good t'know ya!"
The captain wired in he had water comin' in
and the good ship and crew was in peril.
And later that night when 'is lights went outta sight
came the wreck of the *Edmund Fitzgerald*.

Does anyone know where the love of God goes
when the words turn the minutes to hours?
The searchers all say they'd have made Whitefish Bay
if they'd fifteen more miles behind 'er.
They might have split up or they might have capsized;
they may have broke deep and took water.
And all that remains is the faces and the names
of the wives and the sons and the daughters.

Lake Huron rolls, Superior sings
in the rooms of her ice-water mansion.
Old Michigan steams like a young man's dreams;
the islands and bays are for sportsmen.
And farther below Lake Ontario
takes in what Lake Erie can send her.
And the iron boats go as the mariners all know
with the Gales of November remembered.

In a musty old hall in Detroit they prayed,
in the "Maritime Sailors' Cathedral."
The church bell chimed 'til it rang twenty-nine times
for each man on the *Edmund Fitzgerald*.
The legend lives on from the Chippewa on down
of the big lake they call "Gitche Gumee."
"Superior," they say, "never gives up her dead
when the gales of November come early!"

CHAPTER SEVEN

ICE AGE RELIC
IN OUR TIME

LAKE SCIENTISTS estimate that it takes about four hundred years for a drop of water entering the western end of Lake Superior to reach the St. Marys River at its eastern end. Thus, some of the waters passing through the Soo locks today, though depleted by evaporation and supplemented by rain and snowfall, began their passage across the lake about the time that the English were settling Jamestown and Plymouth.

The journey of one such droplet—slipping into the lake out of the St. Louis River and drifting slowly on a gentle current and west wind—would have been a very lonely one for the first century or so. Its first contact with something solid might have been a birch canoe, paddled by a pair of Ojibwe and loaded with wild rice from the sloughs around Chequamegon Bay. Perhaps fifty years later it was part of a giant wave that drove a fur-laden schooner onto the Keweenaw's rocky shore. Another century passed, and it was whipped into a froth of air bubbles by the screw propeller of an ore boat off Au Sable Point. Then, after another half century that could be only yesterday, the droplet encountered its first pollution as it drifted into Whitefish Bay—a drop of oil and a collection of coliform bacteria from a freighter inbound from Europe with a rusty engine and no onboard sanitary facility. Here was the first indication of the perils to come on its journey through the lower lakes—encountering silt, industrial chemicals, agricultural pesticides, and human wastes—before, after several hundred years more, flowing down the St. Lawrence River into the chill waters of the North Atlantic.

Lake Superior today is actually cleaner and clearer than it was at the end of the Ice Age, when it was so clouded by glacial drift that it could not even sustain fish. It is far less polluted than the lower lakes because its cool climate and infertile environs discourage commercial agriculture and because its lake ports have not grown into densely populated metropolises. Politicians and scientists, moreover, have profited by troubles in the lower lakes, and they are better prepared to combat pollution in the largest of the world's freshwater lakes. To be sure, Lake Superior has had its share of problems in the past hundred years—some that have confounded both scientists and politicians—but, with vigilant guard against alien invaders and regulations to prevent human pollution, there is reason to be optimistic about its future.

The Sea Lamprey Invasion

The sea lamprey is abiding testimony that nature's architect, if such there be, is neither benevolent nor aesthetically tasteful. A saltwater alien, the eel-like lamprey, which can reach a length of two feet, has oxygen-intake gills that are mere holes in the side of its head and a round sucking disc for a mouth. Inside the mouth is a toothlike appendage that the animal uses to cut a hole in its prey in order to suck out blood and body fluids. Its favorite victim is a lake trout of about its own size, and when the lamprey has finished its fiendish work, the fish has only about a 20 percent chance of surviving. A lamprey can kill up to twenty pounds of fish during the twelve to twenty months of its adult life.

Although the lamprey originated in a saltwater sea, it can adapt to a freshwater lake. Even saltwater lampreys, like salmon, have to spawn in freshwater streams. Nearing the end of their adult lives, male and female lampreys ascend a stream and use their toothlike appendages to build a nest of small stones and gravel. The female deposits up to sixty thousand eggs in the nest, and then both male and female die. The barely visible larvae live on algae in the stream for five or six years and then metamorphose into free-swimming juveniles with a sucking disc for a

Two lamprey attached to a lake trout. The sea lamprey has hurt both commercial and sport fishing in Lake Superior, although efforts to control this pest have yielded some success.

mouth. About eight to ten inches in length, they swim into the lake to begin their predatory existence.

Although some scientists think lampreys have been in Lake Ontario ever since the St. Lawrence River was freed of glacial ice some two or three thousand years ago, the first positive identification of a lamprey in the lake occurred in 1835. Since this date was shortly after the New York State barge canal, a branch of the Erie Canal that connected Lake Ontario with the Hudson River, was completed, the best current guess is that the noisome sea invaders reached the Great Lakes via New York harbor and the Hudson River.

Interestingly, the lamprey population failed to thrive in Ontario. Commercial fishermen there did not begin to notice lamprey scars on salmon and trout until the 1880s. One probable explanation is that Ontario for much of the nineteenth century was surrounded by wood-lands, and the well-shaded streams that entered it proved too cold for lamprey spawning. Moreover, Niagara Falls prevented the creatures from penetrating into the upper lakes. It was the Welland canal that enabled them to colonize the upper lakes, locate warm, algae-filled streams for spawning, and bring about an environmental disaster.

Following the War of 1812, the people on the Canadian side of the Niagara River—a mixture of Loyalist refugees from the American Revolution and Scottish and English immigrants—formed a private company to build a canal from Lake Erie to Lake Ontario, bypassing Niagara Falls. Completed in 1829, the forty-mile ditch passed through the village of Welland, Ontario, and obtained supplemental water from the Welland Creek (Chippewa Creek on today's maps, commemorating the 1813 Battle of Chippewa). The canal crossed the Niagara escarpment in a series of locks fed by Twelve Mile Creek, which flowed north into Lake Ontario. Water thus ran both ways from the locks, and the lampreys of Ontario, which swam upstream only to spawn, never went beyond the escarpment. A second and third canal (1845, 1887) built to handle the ever larger freighters carrying ore and grain, utilized the same lock system, and the lampreys remained in Lake Ontario. In 1913, however, a fourth canal was begun, this time with a ditch deep enough to be fed in part by a downstream flow from Lake Erie. The first lamprey was reported on the lake in 1921.

Unlike Ontario, Lake Erie is surrounded by lush prairie farmland on both the American and the Canadian sides. Sun-warmed and algae-filled tributaries flowing into the lake were ideal spawning grounds, and the lamprey moved westward, reaching the Detroit River in 1930. By 1940 Lake Huron's commercial fish harvest had plummeted, and fishermen were calling for help from the federal government. World War II prevented any governmental aid to a beleaguered peacetime industry, but in 1946 both Congress and the Michigan legislature appropriated funds to study the lampreys' reproduction cycle. As a result of this research, and to block spawning lamprey, Michigan began experimenting with weirs on creeks that fed lakes Huron and Michigan. In the meantime, the lamprey swam up the St. Marys River and entered Lake Superior. Superior's commercial catch of lake trout began to decline in 1952 and fell by 90 percent over the next decade. In the same period, traps set to assess the lamprey population increased their catch from one thousand to seventy thousand a year.

In 1948 representatives of the United States and Canada, eight U.S. states, and the province of Ontario formed a committee to begin a program of sea lamprey control. While Michigan and Ontario experimented with physical barriers on streams entering the Great Lakes, the U.S. Fish and Wildlife Service began searching for a chemical (lampricide) that would kill lamprey larvae selectively without harming streams' other aquatic residents. It screened more than six thousand chemicals, most of them involving hydrocarbons with chlorine or fluorine atoms attached, over a period of seven years before it found a couple that worked. These two, which go under the trademark names of TFM and Bayer 73, though not 100 percent effective in killing lamprey larvae, are still the major control agents today.

The two-pronged control effort—mechanical barriers and chemical applications—begun in 1960 dramatically reduced lamprey populations on all the lakes and restored sport fishing for trout and whitefish on Lake Superior. In the 1980s the Great Lakes Fishery Commission, a permanent body formed by convention between the United States and Canada, reduced the amount of lampricide applied to feeder streams in response to public concern about the introduction of poisonous chemicals into the environment. By 1995 the lamprey population of Lake Huron had exploded into the millions, though in other lakes it remained at what the international commission regarded as manageable levels.

A 2006 report by the Great Lakes Fishery Commission indicated that the whitefish population of Lake Superior had returned to mid-nineteenth century levels and that the lake trout population was self-sustaining through natural reproduction. That optimistic report was balanced by an announcement from a U.S. Fish and Wildlife biologist based in Marquette, Michigan, that the lake's lamprey population had increased 23 percent from 2004 to 2005. The war against the alien invader is likely to go on indefinitely.

The Taconite Controversy

By the third decade of the twentieth century, it was evident that the soft-earth iron ore mined in open pits in Minnesota's Mesabi Range might soon become exhausted. The soft ore lay near the center of the range;

the eastern third of the iron range consisted of a quartzlike silicate containing fine particles of iron. Geologists, who named this silicate "taconite," did not think it had any commercial value. In the 1930s, however, Edward W. Davis, a professor at the University of Minnesota's School of Mines, designed a process that reduced the rock to a powder, extracted the iron particles with a magnet, and, using a water paste, formed them into a bullet-like pellet with a higher percentage of iron than earthen hematite.

During World War II, when demand for iron and steel peaked, the nation's major steel companies formed a subsidiary, Reserve Mining Company (so-named because they regarded taconite as a long-range backup source), to design and locate a processing plant. Reserve immediately encountered two problems: Davis's process required large quantities of water, and it produced a massive amount of waste tailings. There were few natural lakes on the iron range, and disposing of the tailings on land would create an unsightly settling basin. To Davis and other researchers at the School of Mines, Lake Superior was the answer. It afforded a limitless supply of water for the refining process, and, they assumed, the tailings deposited in the lake would gradually slide into the deep rift at its bottom. Since the tailings were considered chemically inert, scientists assured state officials that they would not pollute the lake or endanger the water supply of Duluth and Two Harbors.

Reserve built a railroad to bring the rock ore down from the range, and in 1955 it completed construction of a refining plant at Silver Bay. At its inception, the Reserve plant and mines employed twenty-five thousand people, and both state and county officials regarded taconite as the commercial salvation of Minnesota's hardscrabble northeast. State agencies readily granted permits for expansion of Reserve's capacity, and by the late 1960s the shipment of taconite pellets to eastern steel mills exceeded the production of earthen ore. Unfortunately, the tailings did not disappear into the bottom of the lake as expected, instead creating an ugly delta off Silver Bay, offending tourists driving the North Shore highway, U.S. 61.

Increasing public concern regarding the environment during the 1960s led federal and state officials to take a more critical look at Reserve's operations and their effect on Lake Superior. The U.S. Department of the

Tailings from the Silver Bay mining operation left a deep scar on Lake Superior's shore.

Interior issued a report criticizing a plume of "green water" that extended about eighteen miles out from the tailings delta. In 1969 scientists began testing the lake for pollutants that might affect Duluth's drinking water. They discovered that the tailings, which had drifted across the end of the lake to the Wisconsin shore, contained a fibrous silicate similar to asbestos, which was known to cause cancer.

In 1970 the states of Minnesota and Wisconsin, soon to be joined by the newly created federal Environmental Protection Agency, sued Reserve in U.S. district court in St. Paul. They sought an order halting tailing dumping in the lake. Bouncing from district to appeals courts

and back, the suit went on for years. After tailing fibers were discovered
in Duluth's drinking water, the issue centered on public health rather
than on Lake Superior's water quality. In 1974 the federal district judge
issued a final order directing Reserve to cease dumping in the lake and
find a site on land instead. After prolonged negotiations with the state of
Minnesota, Reserve finally agreed to build a pipeline that would carry
its tailings to an interior site seven miles from Silver Bay. Thus ended
one of the century's nastiest pollution controversies.

Reserve went bankrupt in 1986, and its facility at Silver Bay ultimately
fell into the hands of Cleveland Cliffs, the mining company that had
discovered an "iron mountain" near Marquette a half century before.
Duluth officials determined that the taconite fibers in the city's water
supply were not a health hazard. Lake Superior emerged from the bitter
fight with nothing more than an ugly scar on its north shore.

The Invisible Threat

This invisible threat was discovered quite by accident. In the mid-1970s
the U.S. Environmental Protection Agency found troubling amounts
of industrial pollutants in fish harvested from Lake Superior. The level
was low, but it seemed to be lakewide, suggesting a variety of sources.
Suspecting that the pollution came from waste dumps in the interior,
the EPA collected samples of fish from the mouths of streams that fed
into the lake. The samples were almost identical to one another, and
they were not significantly higher in pollutants than fish taken from the
middle of the lake.

In July 1977 Wayland Swain, an EPA scientist, headed a crew on a
research vessel testing the waters around Isle Royale. On the cruise's last
day, they docked at a ranger station in Malone Bay on the island's south
end and spent the evening chatting with the resident park ranger. The
ranger suggested they take a look at the island's inland lakes, formed by
the glacier and surrounded by pristine wilderness. Fish from these lakes,
Swain and his crew realized, would be ideal control samples, a base from
which pollution in the main lake could be measured. The ranger suggested they start with Siskiwit Lake, less than a mile from the station.
The island's largest lake, it is seven miles long, a mile and half wide,

and 150 feet deep. Because it lies in a cup of solid basalt, some sixty feet higher than Lake Superior, it has no known connection with the main lake. Swain and his crew decided to extend their cruise by a day in order to fish Siskiwit Lake. "We were excited," Swain later wrote, "that this wild strain of fish from a remote island site would provide us with data about a pristine wilderness area that might be unique." He added, "We had no idea how unique the data would be."

When Swain received the test results the following December, his first reaction was that the lab had made a mistake. The fatty tissue of the fish he had caught in Lake Siskiwit contained PCBs (polychlorinated biphenyl) at twice the level found in the main lake. The Siskiwit fish also contained measurable amounts of DDT, banned in the United States for more than a decade, and four other man-made organic compounds. Concluding that the contaminants had to come from the atmosphere—poisoned rain or snow—Swain asked park rangers to collect some fresh Isle Royale snow. They did so that December, and tests indicated that the island snow contained five times the level of PCBs found in snow that fell on the city of Duluth.

The region to the west of Lake Superior was an early and quite logical suspect. In 1980 Swain discovered a level of toxaphene in Siskiwit Lake that exceeded even the level of PCBs. Toxaphene, a pesticide initially used on southern cotton crops, had recently been put to use by sunflower growers in the Dakotas. When toxaphene was discovered in significant amounts throughout the Great Lakes, the EPA banned its usage in 1983. The Dakotas could not have been a significant source of DDT or PCBs, however. Current scientific thinking focuses on global air circulation. The toxic rain falling on Lake Superior is probably generated by agricultural and industrial practices in China and Russia. The problem to date has not been resolved—and is perhaps unresolvable.

Preserving Ice Age Gems

Prior to 1916, when the National Park Service was established, all the national parks created by Congress, beginning with Yellowstone in 1872, lay west of the Mississippi River. The movement for a national park system naturally focused on the West because the most spectacular national monuments in need of preservation (such as the Grand Canyon and Yosemite) were still in the public domain. As the conservation movement matured during the Progressive years of Woodrow Wilson's presidency, eastern preservationists pointed to the many unspoiled tracts along the Atlantic coast and Great Lakes that were either in public hands or could be purchased inexpensively. In the year the park service was founded, Congress authorized establishment of the first eastern park, Acadia, on the coast of Maine.

Isle Royale on Lake Superior, with abundant wildlife and a landscape untouched since the Ice Age, was a natural candidate for park status. In 1920 Albert Stoll, Jr., a Detroit journalist, visited Isle Royale and wrote a series of editorials promoting park status for the island. Although Stoll had in mind a state park, Michigan congressman James C. Crampton in 1922 introduced a bill making Isle Royale a national park. Opposition from the fishing and lumbering industries delayed its passage until 1931. By then the Great Smoky Mountains, Virginia's Blue Ridge Mountains (Shenandoah), and Kentucky's Mammoth Cave had been similarly honored, so Isle Royale became the fifth of the eastern National Parks.

Aside from a few fishermen's huts on the shore, most of the land on Isle Royale was in the hands of lumber companies, by either ownership or lease from the state of Michigan. The island, which sustained mostly spruce and hemlock among conifers, had never been intensively lumbered. By the 1930s the only operation was that of the Consolidated Paper Company, which was logging spruce pulpwood from the area around Siskiwit Bay. In July 1936 a fire started near its lumber camp and quickly spread over nearly a quarter of the island. The government had little difficulty acquiring the company's charred wasteland. The Depression-born Civilian Conservation Corps built a park headquarters, ranger stations, fire towers, and campgrounds. The park eventually embraced the entire island and surrounding waters, including some two hundred rocky islets. It is accessible today only by boat and can be explored only by footpath or canoe.

As the dominant animal on Isle Royale, the moose has the biggest impact on the forest environment. Moose are so abundant that their waste has rendered the island's lakes undrinkable. Their favorite food is the bark and twigs of aspen, birch, and mountain ash: as a result, these

Isle Royale is home to peaceful trails, scenic views, and abundant moose.

trees are stunted and overgrazed in the upland areas. However, moose have a welcome symbiotic relationship with beaver and wolves. The beaver dam the runoff streams that feed the lakes, and their ponds provide moose with aquatic plants, another of their favorite foods. When beaver cut down an adult aspen or birch for their winter housing and food, they indirectly supply moose with treetop foliage they could not otherwise reach. By encroaching on the beavers' food supply, moose also prevent beaver from overrunning the island.

Wolves, in turn, limit the moose population. Even though wolves usually hunt in packs, they rarely attack a healthy adult moose, which is quite capable of defending itself with antlers and hooves. Calves and aged or infirm adults are wolves' usual prey, a preference which helps keep the moose herd healthy and prevents it from overpopulating. After a kill, the wolves gorge on the meat and depart to rest themselves. When wolves leave a carcass, even temporarily, other small predators such as red fox come in for a meal. Ravens, which follow a wolf pack during the winter, continue the cleanup. Jays, chickadees, and deer mice finish off the bones and their nourishing marrow. Isle Royale thus achieves an ecological balance of its own, one so special that the island has become an outdoor laboratory for scientists of all kinds.

The south shore of Lake Superior also caught conservationists' eyes in the 1930s. Much of it had the same pristine quality and spectacular rock formations as Isle Royale. Of particular interest was the Michigan shoreline from Grand Marais to Munising, which included the Au Sable Dunes, Twelvemile Beach, and Pictured Rocks, features that had excited awe in travelers since the days of Radisson and Groseilliers. Another potential national park was the Wisconsin shoreline from the wild rice–laden sloughs of the Bad River west to Chequamegon Bay, the Apostle Islands, and the Bayfield Peninsula.

The Depression and World War II prevented both state and national governments from taking any action on the two regions, however. During the hard times of the 1930s, Ashland County acquired through tax delinquency substantial holdings on three of the larger Apostle Islands: Stockton, Oak, and Basswood. In the prosperous postwar period, the deer and bear populations of the Apostle Islands captured the attention of Wisconsin hunters. Under their pressure, the state in 1959 purchased Stockton Island and added it to the state forest system. County and state forests were thus the only public holdings on the south shore of Lake Superior when the 1958 election of Gaylord Nelson as governor of Wisconsin gave new momentum to the drive to preserve the region as national park, monument, or forest.

VISITING HISTORY

Northshore Mining Company (Silver Bay, Minnesota) is still in operation, and Cleveland Cliffs Company, which owns the taconite plant, has built a mile-long loop of hiking trail on the hillside, providing vistas of the harbor and the lake. Overlooks identify landmarks and interpret the scene.

Apostle Islands National Lakeshore Headquarters (Bayfield, Wisconsin) contains a Visitors Center for information and permits relative to the islands. In summer, the Apostle Islands Cruise Service in Bayfield offers three-hour narrated boat excursions through the islands.

As governor, Nelson persuaded the Wisconsin legislature to set up a special fund for the acquisition and maintenance of state parks and forests financed by a windshield-sticker user fee of two dollars. He also created an outdoor recreation program, financed by a tax on cigarettes, to improve park facilities. Realizing that acquisition of the Apostle Islands was beyond even these state resources, Nelson in 1961 asked the National Park Service to become involved in preserving the Apostle Islands.

That request reawakened a controversy that had divided conservationists since the turn of the century. Preservationists, whose hero was John Muir, founder of the Sierra Club, argued for preservation of wilderness in its pristine state as a natural wonder, to be seen by human eyes but not touched by human hands. Conservationists, their model Gifford Pinchot, Theodore Roosevelt's chief forester, pled for the discreet use of the public domain, allowing grazing, lumbering, and mining on public lands so long as the exploitation was not wasteful. The controversy, while never resolved, resulted in a distinction between parks, where human usage was limited to short-term visits and sightseeing, and forests, where the government (state or federal) allowed hunting and fishing as well as regulated lumbering and mining.

The problem was that neither Wisconsin's Apostle Islands nor Michigan's Pictured Rocks fell neatly into either category. In Michigan, the littoral itself stood in need of legal protection. Back from the shore, small lakes and wetlands dominated the landscape, preventing construction of roads or other park facilities. State and county roads paralleling the shoreline adhered to the highlands some five or ten miles back from the shore. Michigan's Lake Superior State Forest adequately protected the interior.

The Chequamegon Bay–Apostle Islands tract was even more complicated. Two of the areas that Governor Nelson wanted included in a park—the sloughs of the Bad River and the red sandstone cliffs of Bayfield Peninsula—were on Ojibwe Indian reservations. Given the century-long history of government betrayal, the Ojibwe were understandably leery of placing their lands under park service regulation. In addition, prior to the Indian Reorganization Act of 1934, the Ojibwe had sold parcels of their reservations to whites for summer cottages. The white landowners were even more adamant than the Indians in their opposition to a national park. Further, summer cottage owners on several of the Apostle Islands would have to be bought out in any sort of preservation movement. Madeline Island, largest of the Apostles, was too well populated to even rate consideration as a park.

The idea of a national seashore, a relatively new concept in the never-ending debate over conservation, offered a potential model for the Lake Superior shoreline. In 1937 Congress approved legislation designating Cape Hatteras on North Carolina's Outer Banks a "national seashore recreational area." The basic purpose was to protect Hatteras and related islands in the Outer Banks from commercial or residential development. The islands were essentially sand dunes created when the sea level fell during the Ice Age. If the sea oats and other vegetation holding the dunes were removed, the islands would simply wash into the sea. Although simple preservation was the basic purpose, the statute allowed nonintrusive recreational activities, such as swimming, boating, and fishing. Congress, rich in concepts and niggardly with funding, left land acquisition to the state and to private foundations. As a result, formal establishment of the Cape Hatteras National Seashore was delayed until 1953. To reduce expenses, state officials excluded from the park boundary a half dozen fishing villages on the Pamlico Sound side of the islands.

In the meantime, Congress seemed to forget all about its innovative seashore concept. It did not return to the subject until 1961, when it created the Cape Cod National Seashore. This step actually provided a better model for Lake Superior than did the Hatteras experiment. It offered a milestone in the national conservation movement's history as Congress for the first time authorized federal funding to buy the necessary land for the preserve. Until then, legislation establishing national parks and forests had required that the land be either federally owned or donated to the government.

Cape Cod set another precedent as well. In addition to preserving the cape's sand dunes and beaches (Cape Cod claims the same geological history as do the Outer Banks), officials of the Interior Department thought it necessary to preserve the cape's picturesque historical villages since they were as much a part of the visual attraction as the beaches. The villages were not to be disturbed so long as they had zoning ordinances that met Interior Department standards. Owners of improved property outside the villages were given the option of selling the property and moving or selling it to the government while retaining use rights for life. Similar options were written into the statutes creating Lake Superior's national lakeshores.

Even before the Cape Cod preserve was formally established, the National Park Service was surveying the Great Lakes for places that might fit the seashore model. The survey team concluded that the most promising site was the forty-three miles of Lake Superior shoreline between Grand Marais and Munising, Michigan. Besides the three-hundred-foot-high Au Sable Dunes, the site included the magnificent Pictured Rocks. These cliffs, extending some twelve miles along the lakeshore, were composed of five-hundred-million-year-old sandstone that had been weathered and shaped by wave action. The cliffs are capped by a younger layer of sandstone hardened by calcium that protects them from rapid erosion. As a result, the lake waters have carved out caves at the bottom of the cliffs. Waves slapping into the caves produced a roar that sounded like cannon fire to the French explorer Pierre Esprit Radisson. Groundwater oozing out of cracks in the sandstone left deposits of iron, copper, manganese, and other minerals, producing colorful stains that led to the name *Pictured Rocks*.

In 1961 the park service revealed plans for a National Lakeshore designation for one hundred thousand acres. A park that size would have entailed purchasing large amounts of land, much of it owned by timber companies. As a result, the 1966 law authorizing creation of the Pictured Rocks National Lakeshore represented a compromise on the Cape Cod model. The preserve consisted of two distinct acquisition and management zones. A shoreline zone, in some places no more than a mile wide, would be managed by the park service, preserved in its pristine condition, and used only for public hiking and sightseeing. An inland buffer zone, extending in places some twenty miles into the interior, would be regulated to protect the existing character of the land and the streams that flow into Lake Superior. Managed by private landowners and the state of Michigan, the inland zone allows sustained yield timber harvesting and recreational activities such as hunting and fishing. Pictured Rocks thus became a public treasure with relatively little political controversy. Wisconsin's Apostle Islands sector was another story.

Pictured Rocks National Lakeshore inspires admiration from today's visitors, just as the shoreline did centuries ago.

Having moved from the governorship to the U.S. Senate, Gaylord Nelson in 1965 introduced a bill to create an Apostle Islands National Lakeshore. President Lyndon Johnson, gradually being drawn into the Vietnam War, temporized on congressional expenditures for conservation and called for more study of the Apostle Islands. As a result, congressional hearings on Nelson's bill were delayed until 1967. Because the Indians' attitude was uncertain, the bill did not include any part of Ojibwe reservations; instead, the Indians would be invited to consider participation in the preserve after the National Lakeshore was established. The bill envisioned preservation of the Apostle Islands (except for Madeline Island) as a wilderness but with recreational use. Sport and commercial fishing would be allowed in the summer; hunting and trapping in the fall. The measure finally passed and was signed into law by President Richard Nixon in 1970.

The state of Wisconsin had established an Apostle Islands State Forest in the 1950s, and its Conservation Department (converted to the Department of Natural Resources during Nelson's governorship) began buying out private landowners. By the time the seashore was created in 1970, the state owned 96 percent of Oak and Basswood Islands, and it agreed to manage its holdings in a manner consistent with the National Lakeshore concept. Also by 1970 the Ojibwe attitude toward the lakeshore preserve had become complicated by the national civil rights movement and its offshoot Red Power. When the lakeshore bill came up for final passage in Congress, Indian tribes from as far as California and New Mexico objected on grounds that the bill was depriving Indians of their ancestral lands. After the bill became law, the Ojibwe, long skeptical of federal regulations, declined to allow their reservations to become part of the preserve. Thus, the preserve's boundaries as finally established include only the twenty-one Apostle Islands and fifteen miles of shoreline on the west side of the Bayfield Peninsula.

Canadian efforts to preserve the north shore of Lake Superior paralleled those on the U.S. side. In 1944 the Ontario government established two parks on the lake: Sibley Provincial Park (later Sleeping Giant Provincial Park) on the peninsula that helps form Thunder Bay and Lake Superior Provincial Park at the eastern end of the lake, just north of Sault Ste. Marie. The eastern side of the Sibley Peninsula contains gently rolling lowlands once covered by the waters of glacial Lake Minong and now dotted by remnants of the lake. Park headquarters and a two-hundred-site campground are on the largest of these reservoirs, Marie Louise Lake. The western (Thunder Bay) side of the peninsula, on the other hand, contains huge cliffs, some reaching almost a thousand feet, that loom over the bay. From a distance, the highlands resemble—to those with active imaginations—a "sleeping giant." Ontario renamed the park Sleeping Giant in 1988.

The concept of preserving a pristine wilderness was as slow to develop in Canada as in the United States. Unrestricted lumbering was allowed in both of Ontario's provincial parks until the 1970s. Lake Superior Park remained a wilderness for almost two decades after it was founded simply for lack of road access. The park's sole campground, on the shore at Agawa Bay, was reachable only by boat. Highway 17, the first trans-Canada highway, did not extend to the park until 1960. The first inland campground, with 118 sites, opened the following year. Although Lake Superior Park was classified as a Natural Environment Park in 1967, both it and Sleeping Giant have large campgrounds and receive heavy use by hikers and bicyclists.

Although the dominion government in Ottawa founded a national park as early as 1885—the Banff, in the Canadian Rockies—it did not

VISITING HISTORY

The highway cuts through **Lake Superior Provincial Park** (Highway 17, about seventy miles north of Sault Ste. Marie, Ontario), offering lakeshore vistas and access to developed campgrounds.

Pukaskwa National Park (off Highway 17 via Highway 627 from Marathon, Ontario), the only Canadian national park on Lake Superior, is an environmental reserve penetrated by a single road at its northern end. The park is a striking landscape carved out of the Canadian Shield, but its vast interior is accessible only by hiking trails or canoe. The Visitor Center contains the park's only campground.

Pukaskwa National Park preserves the wilderness that once surrounded Lake Superior.

get around to establishing one on Lake Superior until 1983. Pukaskwa National Park is a 720-square-mile preserve on the lake's northeastern shore, just north of Lake Superior Provincial Park. It is a rugged landscape carved out of the Canadian Shield with mountain crests that reach fifteen hundred feet above lake level. Only one road penetrates the wilderness, at the extreme northern end of the park. Otherwise the vast interior is reached only by hiking trail or canoe. Wolves, bears, and moose roam the woodlands, and there is even a small herd of caribou, the farthest south these animals can be found naturally in Ontario.

The question remains as to how successful these preservation efforts have been. What does the future hold for Lake Superior? The recent experience of the Apostle Islands National Lakeshore in Wisconsin may provide a clue.

When the Apostle Islands Lakeshore was first contemplated, Senator Nelson's staff estimated that it might attract nine hundred thousand

visits annually (one person per day equaled a visit). That optimistic pro-
jection assumed that the Bad River sloughs (a fisherman's paradise) and
the spectacular red cliffs of the Bayfield Peninsula would be part of the
preserve. Both attractions remained in Indian hands. From 1990 to 2001
the National Lakeshore received an annual average of only 166,728 visits.
Ironically, the limited usage has served advocates of "deep ecology," who
want the islands preserved as pristine wilderness. Some of the best features of the Ice Age relic that is Lake Superior may be compatible, after
all, with human needs and designs.

SUGGESTIONS FOR
FURTHER READING

THE BEST introduction to the geological formulation of Lake Superior is Jack L. Hough, *Geology of the Great Lakes* (1958). Two recent studies in the field of anthropology throw a great deal of light on the Paleo-Indian people of the upper Great Lakes prior to the discovery of America: Robert A. Birmingham and Leslie E. Eisenberg, *Indian Mounds of Wisconsin* (2000), and Tim Flannery, *The Eternal Frontier: An Ecological History of North America and Its Peoples* (2001). There are several good accounts of the Indians who lived along the shores of Lake Superior in historic times: Harold Hickerson, *The Chippewa and Their Neighbors: A Study in Ethno-History* (1970); Basil Johnston, *Ojibway Heritage* (1976); Thomas Vennum, Jr., *Wild Rice and the Ojibway People* (1988); Richard White, *The Middle Ground: Indians, Empires, and Republics in the Great Lakes Region, 1660–1815* (1991); and Walker D. Wyman, *The Chippewa: A History Over Three Centuries* (1993).

Although dated, Harold A. Innis, *The Fur Trade in Canada: An Introduction to Canadian Economic History* (1930), remains the standard overview of the trade in the Lake Superior region. Also dated, but a delight to read, is Grace Lee Nute's description of a trader's life, *The Voyageur* (1931). The adventures of Radisson and Groseilliers are told in Peter C. Newman, *Caesars of the Wilderness* (1987).

The mapping expeditions of the 1820s and 1830s are recounted in Arthur M. Woodford, *Charting the Inland Seas: A History of the U.S. Lake Survey* (1994 reprint). There are several good accounts of the copper mining era: Larry Lankton, *Cradle to Grave: Life, Work, and Death in the Lake Superior Copper Mines* (1991); David J. Krause, *The Making of a Mining District: Keweenaw Native Copper, 1500–1870* (1992); and Arthur W. Thurner, *Strangers and Sojourners: History of Michigan's Keweenaw Peninsula* (1994). Theodore Karamanski, *Deep Woods Frontier: A History of Logging in Northern Michigan* (1989), assesses the rather limited timber industry on Lake Superior, and Harlan Hatcher, *A Century of Iron and Men* (1950), describes the westward movement of iron mining, from Michigan to Minnesota. Margaret Bogue, *Fishing the Great Lakes: An Environmental History* (2000), is an exhaustive study of that industry. The Soo Canal, which gave these industries access to world markets, is the subject of John N. Dickinson, *To Build a Canal: Sault Ste. Marie, 1853–1854, and After* (1981).

Accounts of ships and shipwrecks on Lake Superior are too numerous to count. One might start with James Barry, *Ships of the Great Lakes: 300 Years of Navigation* (1973). Also recommended are James R. Marshall, *Shipwrecks of Lake Superior* (2005), and Frederick Stonehouse, *Wreck Ashore: United States Lifesaving Service, Legendary Heroes of the Great Lakes* (1994).

Several books recount the environmental controversies of the twentieth century: Tom Kuchenberg and Jim Legault, *Reflections in a Tarnished Mirror: The Use and Abuse of the Great Lakes* (1978); William Ashworth, *The Late, Great Lakes: An Environmental History* (1986); and Terence Kehoe, *Cleaning Up the Great Lakes: From Cooperation to Confrontation* (1997). George C. Becker, *Fishes of Wisconsin* (1983), discusses the sea lamprey crisis. Harold C. Jordahl, *The Apostle Islands* (1994), traces the political history of Wisconsin's national lakeshore. The best summary of the history and description of other parks around the lake, in both the U.S. and Canada, is to be found in Hugh E. Bishop, *Lake Superior: The Ultimate Guide to the Region* (2005).

INDEX

PICTURE CREDITS

Shining Big Sea Water was designed and set in type
by Dennis Anderson, in Duluth, Minnesota,
nearby Lake Superior. The types are Centaur and Minion.
Printed by Friesens, Altona, Manitoba